OXFORD PICTURE DICTIONARY

Content Areas for Kids

English/Spanish

Jenni Currie Santamaria
Joan Ross Keyes

Program Consultant
Kate Kinsella

OXFORD
UNIVERSITY PRESS

OXFORD
UNIVERSITY PRESS

198 Madison Avenue
New York, NY 10016 USA

Great Clarendon Street, Oxford, OX2 6DP, United Kingdom

Oxford University Press is a department of the University of Oxford.
It furthers the University's objective of excellence in research, scholarship,
and education by publishing worldwide. Oxford is a registered trade
mark of Oxford University Press in the UK and in certain other countries

© Oxford University Press 2012

The moral rights of the author have been asserted

First published in 2012

2 3 4 5 6 7 8 9 10   17 16 15 14 13 12

Library of Congress Cataloging-in-Publication Data

Santamaria, Jenni Currie.
Oxford picture dictionary for content areas for kids : English / Spanish /
Jenni Currie Santamaria, Joan Ross Keyes ; program consultant, Kate Kinsella.
– 2nd ed.
  p. cm.
 Text in English and Spanish.
"Accelerates academic language development."
Joan Ross Keyes was author of the previous edition.
1. Picture dictionaries, Spanish–Juvenile literature. 2. English
language–Dictionaries, Juvenile–Spanish. I. Keyes, Joan Ross. II.
Kinsella, Kate. III. Title.
 PC4629.K49 2012
 423'.17–dc23

             2011036977

No unauthorized photocopying

All rights reserved. No part of this publication may be reproduced, stored
in a retrieval system, or transmitted, in any form or by any means, without
the prior permission in writing of Oxford University Press, or as expressly
permitted by law, by licence or under terms agreed with the appropriate
reprographics rights organization. Enquiries concerning reproduction outside
the scope of the above should be sent to the ELT Rights Department, Oxford
University Press, at the address above

You must not circulate this work in any other form and you must impose
this same condition on any acquirer

Links to third party websites are provided by Oxford in good faith and for
information only. Oxford disclaims any responsibility for the materials
contained in any third party website referenced in this work

Executive Publishing Manager: Stephanie Karras
Managing Editor: Marni Sabin
Associate Development Editor: Charlotte Roh
Art and Design Director: Susan Sanguily
Executive Design Manager: Maj Hagsted
Designer: Sangeeta E. Ramcharan
Electronic Production Manager: Julie Armstrong
Production Artist: Elissa Santos
Cover Design: Molly Scanlon
Senior Image Manager: Trisha Masterson
Image Editor: Fran Newman
Production Coordinator: Kathy Lovisolo
Senior Manufacturing Controller: Eve Wong

ISBN: 978 0 19 401777 0

Printed in China

This book is printed on paper from certified and well-managed sources

ACKNOWLEDGEMENTS

Illustrations by: Scott Angle: 110-111, 144-145; Lalena Fisher: 32 (bot.), 33 (top),
54 (bot.), 55 (top), 80 (bot.), 81 (top), 90(bot.), 91 (top), 104 (bot.), 105 (top), 124
(bot.), 125 (top), 128-129, 136 (bot.), 137 (top), 154 (bot.), 155 (top), 158-159, 168
(bot.), 169 (top); Ken Gamage: 7; Leslie Harrington: 12-13, 14-15, 16-17, 18-19,
20-21, 22-23, 24-25, 26-27, 28-29, 30-31, 34-35, 36-37, 38-39, 40-41, 42-43, 44-45,
46-47, 164-165; Nathan Jarvis: 78-79, 88-89, 138-139, 146-147, 152-153, 156-157;
John Kaufmann: 140-141, 148-149; Shawn McKelvey: 56-57, 60-61, 62-63, 68-69,
70-71, 82-83, 108-109, 130-131, 132-133, 142-143; Jorge Santillan: 6, 8-9, 10-11,
48-49, 50-51, 52-53, 150-151; Scott Seibel: 58-59, 72-73, 74-75; Ben Shannon:
64-65, 66-67, 76-77, 84-85, 86-87, 92-93, 94-95, 96-97, 98-99, 100-101, 102-103,
106-107, 112-113, 126-127, 134-135, 160-161, 162-163, 166-167; Sam Tomasello:
114-115, 116-117, 118-119, 120-121, 122-123; Sam Ward: 5;
Back cover: Shortkut/shutterstock.com (laptop).

Cover Illustrator: Leslie Harrington
Cover Design: Molly K. Scanlon

Acknowledgments

Series Consultant

Kate Kinsella, Ed.D., has a rich and varied background teaching youth and writing curricula to support their English language and literacy growth. She completed her doctorate in second language acquisition and multicultural education at the University of San Francisco, where she accepted a faculty position in San Francisco State University's Center for Teacher Efficacy. A highly sought after teacher educator and program advisor, she provides training and consultancy nationally to state departments, districts, and individual schools. She stays actively involved teaching English Learners across the K–12 grade levels, providing in-class lesson demonstrations and coaching. A former TESOL Fulbright scholar, Dr. Kinsella has served as the editor of the CATESOL Journal and as the chief K–12 editor on the TESOL Journal. Dr. Kinsella has also served as the pedagogical guide for numerous English learner programs and dictionaries, including the *Oxford Picture Dictionary for the Content Areas*. She plans to dedicate the next decade of her professional life to creating engaging, relevant curricula that enables teachers to advance English language and literacy for immigrant youths so they exit secondary school both college and career ready.

Assessment Expert

Margo Gottlieb, Ph.D., is a national expert in the design of assessments for English Language Learners, in the evaluation of language education programs, and in the development of English language proficiency standards in pre-K–12 settings. Currently, she is Director of Assessment and Evaluation for the Illinois Resource Center and Lead Developer for the World-Class Instructional Design and Assessment (WIDA) Consortium at the Wisconsin Center for Education Research at the University of Wisconsin. Margo has a Ph.D. in Public Policy Analysis, Evaluation Research and Program Design, an M.A. in Applied Linguistics, and a B.A. in the teaching of Spanish. She has published an extensive array of materials, including monographs, handbooks, books, and a dozen book chapters.

Authors

Jenni Currie Santamaria holds an MFA in TEFL/ESL and has been working with English learners of various ages and levels since 1989. She has served as an ESL instructor, technology mentor, curriculum developer, and teacher trainer. Her publications include numerous interactive materials and teaching guides, including the lesson plans for the *Oxford Picture Dictionary*.

Joan Ross Keyes is a former ESL teacher with more than 20 years of classroom experience in both elementary and junior high schools. Joan has facilitated ESL workshops around the country and was also an adjunct professor at Long Island University for many years. Her passion for teaching English learners contributed to the success of the original *Oxford Picture Dictionary for Kids*.

National Standards and Content Area Consultants

Social Studies Expert

Jeff Passe, Ph.D., is Chair of the Department of Secondary Education at Towson University in Maryland. He specializes in curriculum and social studies. A former elementary school teacher, he is the author of five books and dozens of chapters and articles. His research primarily focuses on the teaching of current events. In 2008, he completed his term on the Board of Directors of the National Council for the Social Studies, highlighted by his presidency from 2005–2006.

Science Expert

Julie A. Luft, Ph.D., is a Professor of Science Education at Arizona State University at Tempe, Fulton Graduate School of Education, and Research Director for the National Science Teachers Association. She has been the professional investigator of several professional development and research grants. Dr. Luft has served as president and board member of the Association for Science Teacher Education, on the Board of the National Science Teachers Association, and she has been Associate Editor for several journals.

Math Expert

Vena M. Long, Ed.D., is a Professor of Mathematics Education and Associate Dean for Research and Professional Development at the University of Tennessee. Dr. Long served on the Board of Directors of the National Council of Teachers of Mathematics from 2006–2010 and is also active in local- and state-level professional organizations.

Our Advisory Committee

English Learner Expert

Linda New Levine, Ph.D., is a consultant with the Center for Applied Linguistics. She advises teachers of English language learning children and programs for teaching English as a Foreign Language in both primary and secondary classrooms. She has been a teacher of English as a Second Language in K–12 classrooms and a Staff Development Facilitator for the Bedford Central School district in New York. She was also an adjunct assistant professor of ESL Methods and Materials at Teachers College, Columbia University.

Literacy Expert

Charlene Cobb, Ed.D., is Executive Director for Teaching and Learning in East Maine School District 63 in Des Plaines, Illinois. Over the past twenty years she has worked nationally with schools and districts to support literacy programs as a teacher, reading specialist, professor, consultant, and an advocate across all domains of content. She is particularly interested in the literacy development of linguistically diverse learners and struggling readers, and believes that building background knowledge through the development of academic vocabulary is critical to closing the achievement gap.

Special Education Expert

Donnalyn Jaque-Anton is an educational consultant working with schools and districts on the integration of general and special education and response to intervention and instruction to ensure academic achievement for all students. She brings years of practical experience as a teacher at all levels, a principal, and as a district administrator. As the former Executive Officer of Los Angeles Unified School District (LAUSD), she implemented a visionary plan for students with disabilities (Schools for All Children) which erased the culture of failure for that group of "at risk" students in the nation's second largest school district.

The publisher and author would like to acknowledge the following individuals for their invaluable feedback during the development of this program.

Sandra Garnett: Albany County School District #1, WY

Patricia Milazzo: Alief ISD, TX

Ronald DeFalco: Bellwood District 88, IL

Linda Camerino: Bladen County Schools, NC

Mary E. Kaiser: Blaine County School District, ID

Kathryn Mizuno: Camden City School District, NJ

Catherine Fox: Central Falls School District, RI

Lisa Marie Lewis, Siobhan Lavin Mulvey: Charlotte-Mecklenburg Schools, NC

Griselda E. Flores: Chicago Public Schools, IL

Blaire Brandon, Jessica Maston: Clayton County Public Schools, GA

Camelia Courtright, Vicki Sue Steenhoek: Cobb County School District, GA

Sarah Rowan: Copiague UFSD, NY

Klodia Ibrahim: Dearborn Public Schools, MI

Nancy Foskey: DeKalb County School System, GA

Diann Mackey: Des Moines Public Schools, IA

Mary Beth Scott: Downingtown Area School District, PA

Catherine Spencer: East Allen County Schools, IN

Katherine Zlogar: East Maine District 63, IL

Pam Garvie: Enid Public Schools, OK

Huong Banh: Evanston/Skokie District 65, IL

Doris Cook, Nancy Ellen Cook: Fort Worth ISD, TX

Jennifer Sijmons: Greenwich Public Schools, CT

Felicia Bundy: Guilford County Public Schools, NC

Johanna McPhee: Hampton School District, NH

Gail Cogdill: Harnett County Schools, NC

Patsy Mills: Houston ISD, TX

Esmeralda Polanco: Irving ISD, TX

Charlotte Johnson: Lebanon School District, NH

Stacy Rowan: Lewisville ISD, TX

Amy S. Cochran: Metropolitan Nashville Public Schools, TN

Roslyn Eisner, Janet E. Lasky, Ann E. Morgan: Montgomery County Public Schools, MD

Amy Irene Halsall: MSD Warren Township, IN

Lisa Allphin, Joan Doyle: Mt. Diablo USD, CA

Lisa Spencer: Newark Central School District, NY

Misty Campos: Orange USD, CA

Eunice Alvarado-Martinez, Tamara Lopez, Enrique Rivera-Torres, Carmen S. Santiago: Orange County Public Schools, FL

Rita Tantillo: Paradise Valley USD, AZ

Maureen Carmody, Alison Garcia: Patchogue-Medford UFSD, NY

Mary E. McConville: Pittsford School District, NY

Beth Anderson: Plano ISD, TX

Lisa Rinehart: Plano CUSD 88, IL

Edie Thompson: Purdy R-II School District, MO

Patricia Lewno: Racine USD, WI

Anna R. Ferro: Rochester City School District, NY

Fiona Lyons: Rye Neck School District, NY

Kristine B. Heim: Saint Paul Public Schools, MN

Eileen Marchetti: Shenandoah Valley School District, PA

Sarah Steele: Warsaw Community Schools, IN

Anne Hagerman Wilcox: Wendell School District, ID

Mèlanie R. Álvarez: White Plains Public Schools, NY

Letter to Students

Hello! My name is Dr. Kate Kinsella. I'm a professor who helps many people become excellent teachers. I helped with this amazing picture dictionary. I know it will help you learn many useful new words.

My own son, John Carlos, is an English learner like you! He was born in Guatemala and he speaks Spanish. He loves looking at the beautiful and exciting pictures. At home, he likes to play "I Spy" with his sister, Jane Dzung, to find new words in the big picture. At school, he has fun working with a partner to practice using the new words.

At first, some words may seem difficult. Don't worry! I know if you say, read, and write the words often, you will become a terrific English speaker just like my son. I believe in you!

All my best,

Dr. Kate

How to Use this Dictionary

Topic Pages

These pages teach you new words with a big picture. You will look at the big picture, read new words, and have interesting things to talk about.

This box tells you the topic number.

This box tells you the topic name.

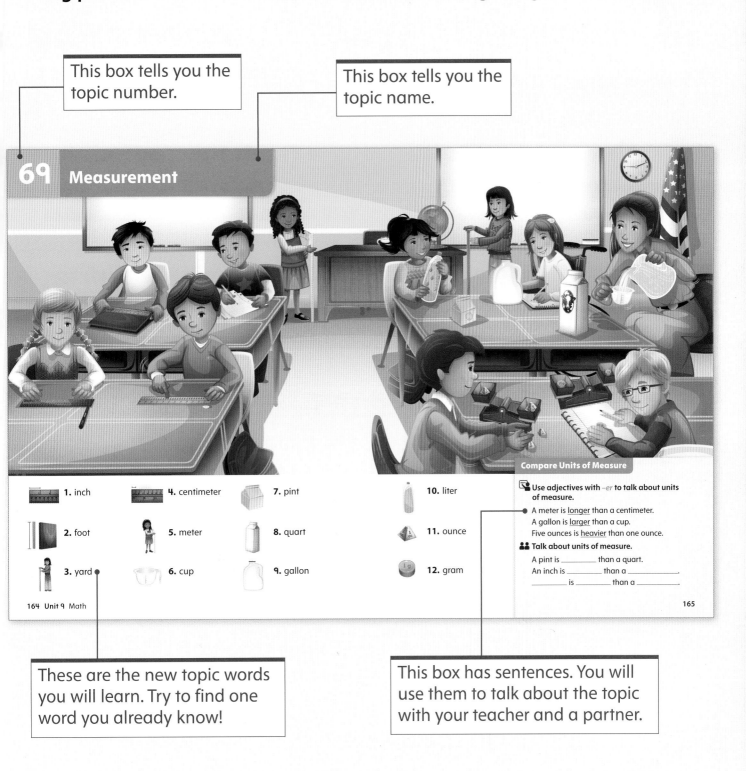

69 Measurement

1. inch	4. centimeter	7. pint	10. liter
2. foot	5. meter	8. quart	11. ounce
3. yard	6. cup	9. gallon	12. gram

164 Unit 9 Math

Compare Units of Measure

Use adjectives with –er to talk about units of measure.

- A meter is <u>longer</u> than a centimeter.
  A gallon is <u>larger</u> than a cup.
  Five ounces is <u>heavier</u> than one ounce.

Talk about units of measure.

A pint is _____ than a quart.
An inch is _____ than a _____.
_____ is _____ than a _____.

165

These are the new topic words you will learn. Try to find one word you already know!

This box has sentences. You will use them to talk about the topic with your teacher and a partner.

vii

Unit Opening Pages

These pages are at the beginning of each unit. They have useful words that you will need in school, at home, and in your community.

Each word or phrase has a picture to show you what it means.

11 A Day at School

1. read

2. write

7. work with a partner

8. work in a group

3. draw

4. repeat

9. ask questions

10. answer questions

5. think

6. raise hand

Discuss School Activities

Use the verb *does* to ask questions about the students.

A: What <u>does</u> Alex do at school?
B: He reads.

B: What <u>does</u> Jasmine do at school?
A: She works in a group.

A: What <u>does</u> Tyler do at school?
B: He answers questions.

Ask and answer questions about the students at school.

A: What _____ Elena do at school?
B: She writes.

B: What does _____ do at school?
A: _____

The word in color shows you the language skill that you will learn.

Unit Expansion Pages

These pages are at the end of each unit. Your teacher will help you with activities to use the unit words in new ways.

These are charts. You will use the charts to organize words from the unit.

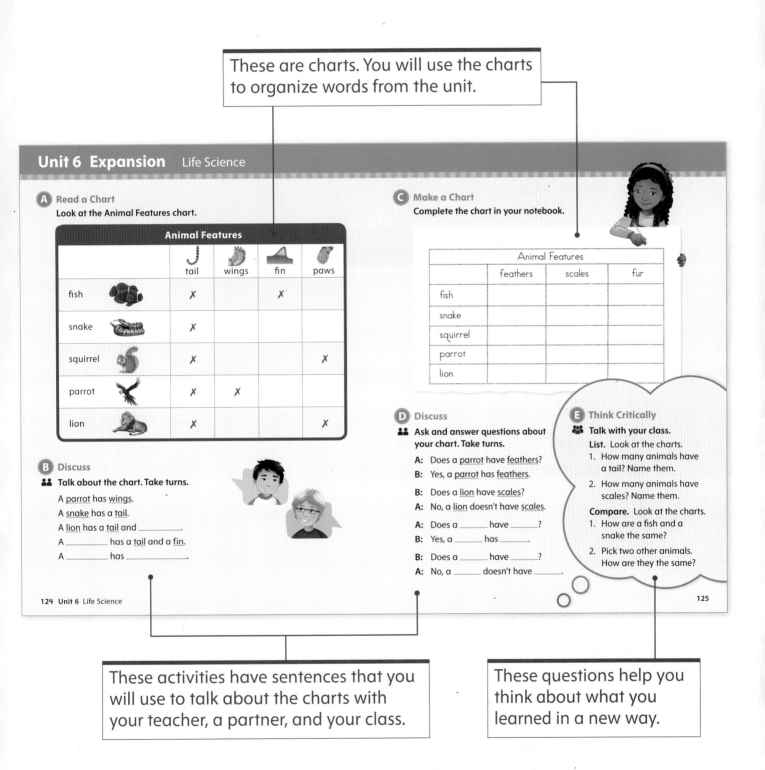

Unit 6 Expansion Life Science

A Read a Chart
Look at the Animal Features chart.

Animal Features

		tail	wings	fin	paws
fish		✗		✗	
snake		✗			
squirrel		✗			✗
parrot		✗	✗		
lion		✗			✗

B Discuss
Talk about the chart. Take turns.

A <u>parrot</u> has <u>wings</u>.
A <u>snake</u> has a <u>tail</u>.
A <u>lion</u> has a <u>tail</u> and _____.
A _____ has a <u>tail</u> and a <u>fin</u>.
A _____ has _____.

C Make a Chart
Complete the chart in your notebook.

Animal Features			
	feathers	scales	fur
fish			
snake			
squirrel			
parrot			
lion			

D Discuss
Ask and answer questions about your chart. Take turns.

A: Does a <u>parrot</u> have <u>feathers</u>?
B: Yes, a <u>parrot</u> has <u>feathers</u>.

B: Does a <u>lion</u> have <u>scales</u>?
A: No, a <u>lion</u> doesn't have <u>scales</u>.

A: Does a _____ have _____?
B: Yes, a _____ has _____.

B: Does a _____ have _____?
A: No, a _____ doesn't have _____.

E Think Critically
Talk with your class.
List. Look at the charts.
1. How many animals have a tail? Name them.
2. How many animals have scales? Name them.

Compare. Look at the charts.
1. How are a fish and a snake the same?
2. Pick two other animals. How are they the same?

These activities have sentences that you will use to talk about the charts with your teacher, a partner, and your class.

These questions help you think about what you learned in a new way.

Table of Contents Contenido

Getting Started Para comenzar

Numbers Los números	2
Ordinal Numbers Los números ordinales	4
Calendars El calendario	5
Times La hora	6
Colors Los colores	7
Opposites Los opuestos	8
Prepositions Las preposiciones	10

Unit 1 At Home En casa

1	Every Day Día a día	12
2	Friends Los amigos	14
3	Family La familia	16
4	Home La casa	18
5	The Bedroom La recámara	20
6	The Bathroom El cuarto de baño	22
7	Breakfast in the Kitchen El desayuno en la cocina	24
8	The Living Room La sala de estar	26
9	Everyday Clothes La ropa de todos los días	28
10	Seasonal Clothes La ropa según las estaciones	30
	Unit Expansion: At Home	32

Unit 2　At School　En la escuela

11	A Day at School Un día en la escuela	34
12	The School La escuela	36
13	School Supplies Los útiles escolares	38
14	The Classroom El salón de clases	40
15	The Library La biblioteca	42
16	The Computer Lab El laboratorio de computación	44
17	Lunch in the Cafeteria El almuerzo en la cantina	46
18	Physical Education Educación física	48
19	The Nurse's Office La enfermería	50
20	Feelings Los sentimientos	52
Unit Expansion: At School		54

Unit 3　Community　La comunidad

21	People at Work La gente en el trabajo	56
22	The Neighborhood El vecindario	58
23	The Community La comunidad	60
24	Businesses in Town Las tiendas de la ciudad	62
25	The Supermarket El supermercado	64
26	The Restaurant El restaurante	66
27	The City La ciudad	68
28	Transportation El transporte	70
29	The Harbor El puerto	72
30	The Hospital El hospital	74
31	Fire Safety Prevención de incendios	76
32	The Farm La granja	78
Unit Expansion: Community		80

Unit 4 The United States Los Estados Unidos

33 Biography Verbs Los verbos de las biografías   82

34 Map Skills Destrezas en el mapa   84

35 The Government El gobierno   86

36 American Symbols Los símbolos de los Estados Unidos   88

Unit Expansion: The United States   90

Unit 5 Health Salud

37 Healthy Habits Hábitos saludables   92

38 Faces La cara   94

39 Parts of the Body Las partes del cuerpo   96

40 More Parts of the Body Más partes del cuerpo   98

41 The Senses Los sentidos   100

42 Nutrition La nutrición   102

Unit Expansion: Health   104

Unit 6   Life Science   Ciencias de la vida

43   Observe and Measure Observar y medir   106

44   Plants Las plantas   108

45   Animals in the Zoo Los animales del zoológico   110

46   Growing and Changing Crecer y cambiar   112

47   The Ocean El océano   114

48   The Desert El desierto   116

49   The Forest El bosque   118

50   The Rain Forest La selva tropical   120

51   The Grassland La pradera   122

Unit Expansion: Life Science   124

Unit 7   Physical Science   Ciencias físicas

52   Experiment and Record Experimentar y registrar   126

53   Matter La materia   128

54   Heat, Light, and Sound El calor, la luz y el sonido   130

55   Motion and Force El movimiento y la fuerza   132

56   Energy and Electricity La energía y la electricidad   134

Unit Expansion: Physical Science   136

Unit 8 Earth and Space Science La Tierra y la ciencia espacial

57 Land and Water La tierra y el agua — 138

58 In the Mountains En la montaña — 140

59 Earth Materials Los materiales de la Tierra — 142

60 Dinosaurs and Fossils Los dinosaurios y los fósiles — 144

61 Weather El clima — 146

62 On the Coast En la costa — 148

63 The Environment El medio ambiente — 150

64 Space El espacio — 152

Unit Expansion: Earth and Space Science — 154

Unit 9 Math Matemática

65 Telling Time La hora — 156

66 Math Words Términos matemáticos — 158

67 Shapes Las figuras y los cuerpos geométricos — 160

68 Fractions and Decimals Las fracciones y los decimales — 162

69 Measurement La medición — 164

70 Money El dinero — 166

Unit Expansion: Math — 168

Meet the Kids

Alex

Elena

Jasmine

Tyler

Getting Started

Numbers

Los números

1	one	•	uno
2	two	• •	dos
3	three	• • •	tres
4	four	• • • •	cuatro
5	five	• • • • •	cinco
6	six	• • • • • •	seis
7	seven	• • • • • • •	siete
8	eight	• • • • • • • •	ocho
9	nine	• • • • • • • • •	nueve
10	ten	• • • • • • • • • •	diez
11	eleven	• • • • • • • • • • •	once
12	twelve	• • • • • • • • • • • •	doce
13	thirteen	• • • • • • • • • • • • •	trece
14	fourteen	• • • • • • • • • • • • • •	catorce
15	fifteen	• • • • • • • • • • • • • • •	quince
16	sixteen	• • • • • • • • • • • • • • • •	dieciséis
17	seventeen	• • • • • • • • • • • • • • • • •	diecisiete
18	eighteen	• • • • • • • • • • • • • • • • • •	dieciocho
19	nineteen	• • • • • • • • • • • • • • • • • • •	diecinueve
20	twenty	• • • • • • • • • • • • • • • • • • • •	veinte

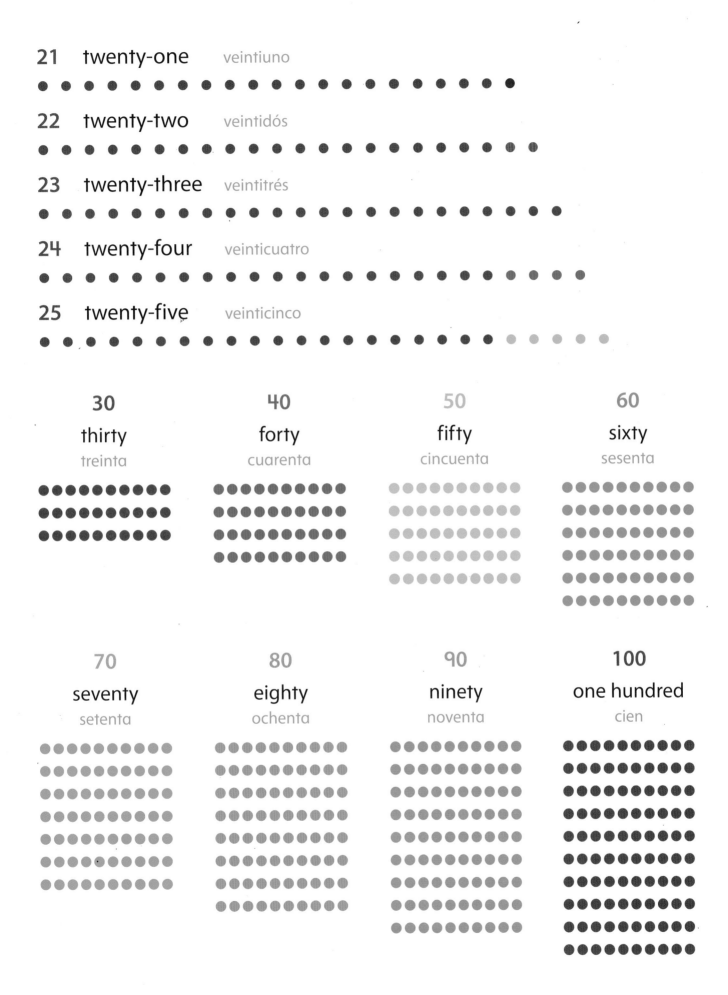

21 twenty-one   *veintiuno*

22 twenty-two   *veintidós*

23 twenty-three   *veintitrés*

24 twenty-four   *veinticuatro*

25 twenty-five   *veinticinco*

30 thirty *treinta*	**40** forty *cuarenta*	**50** fifty *cincuenta*	**60** sixty *sesenta*
70 seventy *setenta*	**80** eighty *ochenta*	**90** ninety *noventa*	**100** one hundred *cien*

Ordinal Numbers

Los números ordinales

1st first primer/o/a	★	☆	☆	☆	☆	☆	☆	☆	☆	☆
2nd second segundo/a	☆	★	☆	☆	☆	☆	☆	☆	☆	☆
3rd third tercer/o/a	☆	☆	★	☆	☆	☆	☆	☆	☆	☆
4th fourth cuarto/a	☆	☆	☆	★	☆	☆	☆	☆	☆	☆
5th fifth quinto/a	☆	☆	☆	☆	★	☆	☆	☆	☆	☆
6th sixth sexto/a	☆	☆	☆	☆	☆	★	☆	☆	☆	☆
7th seventh séptimo/a	☆	☆	☆	☆	☆	☆	★	☆	☆	☆
8th eighth octavo/a	☆	☆	☆	☆	☆	☆	☆	★	☆	☆
9th ninth noveno/a	☆	☆	☆	☆	☆	☆	☆	☆	★	☆
10th tenth décimo/a	☆	☆	☆	☆	☆	☆	☆	☆	☆	★

Calendar

El calendario

Days of the Week

Los días de la semana

Sunday domingo	Monday lunes	Tuesday martes	Wednesday miércoles	Thursday jueves	Friday viernes	Saturday sábado
		1	2	3	4	5
6	7	8	9	10	11	12
13	14	15	16	17	18	19

Months of the Year

Los meses del año

January
enero

1	2	3	4	5	6	7
8	9	10	11	12	13	14
15	16	17	18	19	20	21
22	23	24	25	26	27	28
29	30	31				

February
febrero

			1	2	3	4
5	6	7	8	9	10	11
12	13	14	15	16	17	18
19	20	21	22	23	24	25
26	27	28	29			

March
marzo

			1	2	3
4	5	6	7	8	9	10
11	12	13	14	15	16	17
18	19	20	21	22	23	24
25	26	27	28	29	30	31

April
abril

1	2	3	4	5	6	7
8	9	10	11	12	13	14
15	16	17	18	19	20	21
22	23	24	25	26	27	28
29	30					

May
mayo

	1	2	3	4	5
6	7	8	9	10	11	12
13	14	15	16	17	18	19
20	21	22	23	24	25	26
27	28	29	30	31		

June
junio

					1	2
3	4	5	6	7	8	9
10	11	12	13	14	15	16
17	18	19	20	21	22	23
24	25	26	27	28	29	30

July
julio

1	2	3	4	5	6	7
8	9	10	11	12	13	14
15	16	17	18	19	20	21
22	23	24	25	26	27	28
29	30	31				

August
agosto

		1	2	3	4
5	6	7	8	9	10	11
12	13	14	15	16	17	18
19	20	21	22	23	24	25
26	27	28	29	30	31	

September
septiembre

						1
2	3	4	5	6	7	8
9	10	11	12	13	14	15
16	17	18	19	20	21	22
23	24	25	26	27	28	29
30						

October
octubre

	1	2	3	4	5	6
7	8	9	10	11	12	13
14	15	16	17	18	19	20
21	22	23	24	25	26	27
28	29	30	31			

November
noviembre

				1	2	3
4	5	6	7	8	9	10
11	12	13	14	15	16	17
18	19	20	21	22	23	24
25	26	27	28	29	30	

December
diciembre

						1
2	3	4	5	6	7	8
9	10	11	12	13	14	15
16	17	18	19	20	21	22
23	24	25	26	27	28	29
30	31					

Time

La hora

morning

mañana

night

noche

afternoon

tarde

evening

tarde

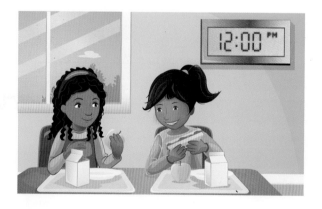

noon

mediodía

midnight

medianoche

Colors

Los colores

red

rojo/a

orange

anaranjado/a

yellow

amarillo/a

green

verde

blue

azul

purple

morado/a

pink

rosado/a

tan

habano

brown

café

black

negro/a

white

blanco/a

gray

gris

Opposites
Los opuestos

small
pequeño/a

large
grande

left
izquierda

right
derecha

new
nuevo/a

old
viejo/a

open
abierto/a

closed
cerrado/a

short
bajo/a

tall
alto/a

slow
lento/a

fast
rápido/a

full
lleno/a

empty
vacío/a

light
liviano/a

heavy
pesado/a

clean
limpio/a

dirty
sucio/a

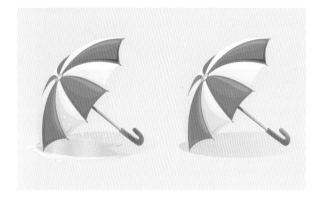

wet
mojado/a

dry
seco/a

cold
frío/a

hot
caliente

same
igual

different
diferente

Prepositions

Las preposiciones

The book is on the box.

El libro está **sobre** la caja.

The book is in the box.

El libro está **en** la caja.

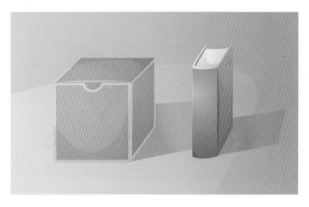

The book is next to the box.

El libro está **al lado de** la caja.

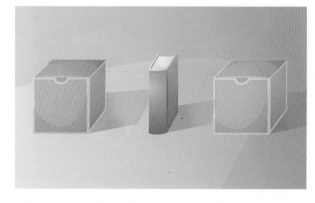

The book is between the boxes.

El libro está **entre** las cajas.

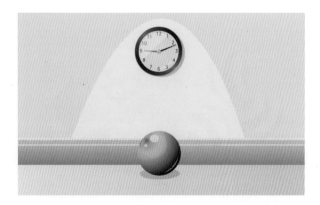

The clock is above the ball.
The ball is below the clock.

El reloj está **encima de** la pelota.
La pelota está **debajo del** reloj.

The girls are in front of the boy.
The boys are behind the girls.

Las niñas están **delante del** niño.
Los niños están **detrás de** las niñas.

The girl is across from the boy.
La niña está **enfrente del** niño.

The ball goes through the hoop.
La pelota pasa **a través del** aro.

The boy goes up the stairs.
El niño va hacia **arriba**.

The girl goes down the stairs.
La niña va hacia **abajo**.

The girl goes around the tree.
La niña pasea **alrededor del** árbol.

The car goes over the bridge.
The boat goes under the bridge.
El carro circula **sobre** el puente.
El barco pasa **bajo** el puente.

1. wake up
despertarse

2. take a shower
ducharse

3. take a bath
bañarse

4. get dressed
vestirse

5. comb hair
peinarse el cabello

6. eat breakfast
desayunar

7. eat dinner
cenar

8. do homework
hacer la tarea

9. brush teeth
cepillarse los dientes

10. go to bed
ir a dormir

Discuss Daily Activities

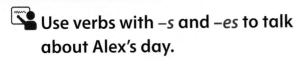 **Use verbs with –s and –es to talk about Alex's day.**

He <u>wakes</u> up at 7:00 a.m.
He <u>gets</u> dressed at 7:30 a.m.

He <u>does</u> homework at 7:00 p.m.
He <u>goes</u> to bed at 8:15 p.m.

Talk about Alex's day.

He _____s his hair at 7:40 a.m.
He _____es his teeth at 8:00 p.m.

He _____ breakfast at _____.
He _____ at _____.

13

2 Friends
Los amigos

Tyler

Alex

 1. eyes
los ojos

 4. hair
el cabello

 7. long
largo/a

 2. eyelashes
las pestañas

 5. bangs
el flequillo

 8. short
corto/a

 3. glasses
los lentes

 6. ponytail
la coleta

 9. straight
lacio/a

Jasmine

Elena

Describe People

10. curly
rizado/a

11. dark
oscuro/a

12. light
claro/a

Use the verb *has* to talk about people.

Alex <u>has</u> bangs.

Jasmine <u>has</u> dark hair.

Talk about the friends.

Elena _____ a ponytail.

Tyler _____ glasses.

She has _____.

He has _____.

15

3 Family
La familia

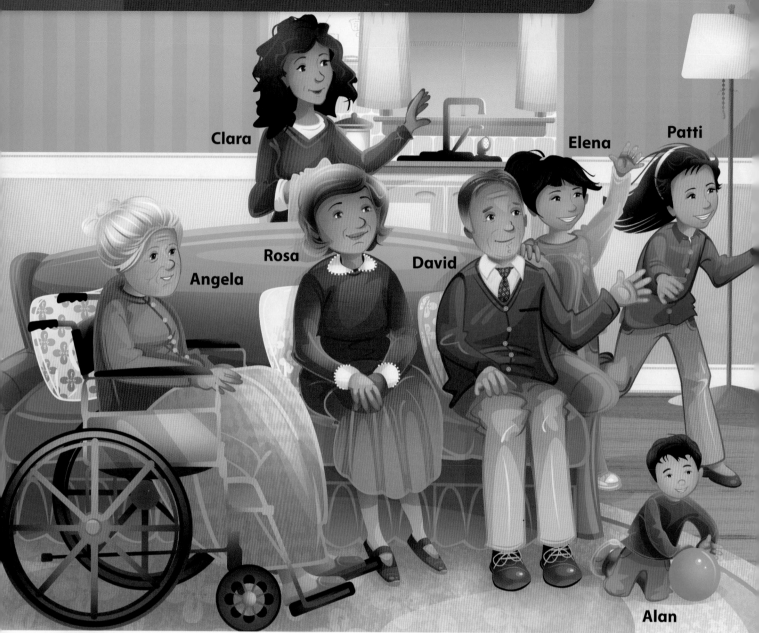

Clara

Elena

Patti

Angela

Rosa

David

Alan

 1. sister
la hermana

 4. father
el padre

 7. grandfather
el abuelo

 2. brother
el hermano

 5. parents
los padres

 8. grandparents
los abuelos

 3. mother
la madre

 6. grandmother
la abuela

 9. great-grandmother
la bisabuela

Martin

Tony

Eva

Angie

Daniel

Identify Family Relationships

10. aunt
la tía

11. uncle
el tío

12. cousin
la prima

Use the verbs *is* and *are* to talk about family.

Patti <u>is</u> her sister.

Angie and Daniel <u>are</u> her cousins.

Talk about Elena's family.

Tony _____ her uncle.

David and Rosa _____ her grandparents.

_____ is her _____.

_____ are her _____.

4 Home

La casa

living room
la sala de estar

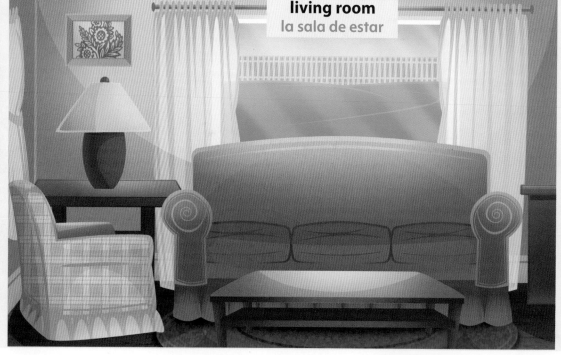

 1. sink
el fregadero

 4. mirror
el espejo

 7. wall
la pared

 2. door
la puerta

 5. picture
el cuadro

 8. stairs
la escalera

 3. lamp
la lámpara

 6. window
la ventana

 9. table
la mesa

bathroom
el cuarto de baño

bedroom
la recámara

kitchen
la cocina

Discuss Things in the Home

10. floor
el piso

11. eat
comer

12. cook
cocinar

Use *There is* _____. and *There are* _____. to talk about things in the home.

There is one window.
There are two sinks.
There are three lamps.

Talk about the things in the home.

There is one _____.
There are two _____.
There is _____.
There are _____.

19

 1. bed
la cama

 4. closet
el armario

 7. drawer
la gaveta

 2. blanket
la manta

 5. dresser
el tocador

 8. alarm clock
el reloj despertador

 3. pillow
la almohada

 6. desk
el escritorio

 9. toys
los juguetes

Describe Location

10. puzzle
el rompecabezas

11. pick up
recoger

12. put away
guardar

Use the prepositions *in, on,* and *under* to talk about where things are.

The toy is <u>in</u> the drawer.
The alarm clock is <u>on</u> the desk.
The puzzle is <u>under</u> the dresser.

Talk about where things are in the bedroom.

The _____ is in the _____.
The _____ is on the _____.
The _____ is under the _____.
The _____ is _____ the _____.

21

6 The Bathroom
El cuarto de baño

1. water
el agua

4. shampoo
el champú

7. toothbrush
el cepillo de dientes

2. bathtub
la bañera

5. soap
el jabón

8. toothpaste
el dentífrico

3. toilet
el inodoro

6. towel
la toalla

9. comb
el peine

Discuss Things People Use

10. brush
cepillarse

11. wash
lavarse

12. dry
secarse

Use the preposition *with* to talk about things people use.

She washes her face <u>with</u> soap.
He brushes his teeth <u>with</u> a toothbrush.
She dries her hands <u>with</u> a towel.

Talk about the things people use in the bathroom.

He washes his hair _____ shampoo.
She combs her hair _____ a comb.
He _____ with _____.
She _____ with _____.

23

7 Breakfast in the Kitchen

El desayuno en la cocina

 1. stove
la cocina

 2. refrigerator
el refrigerador

 3. cabinet
el armario

 4. counter
la encimera

 5. cup
la taza

 6. plate
el plato

 7. eggs
los huevos

 8. grapes
las uvas

 9. bananas
los plátanos

Determine Location

10. butter
la mantequilla

11. bread
el pan

12. cereal
el cereal

Use *Where is* _____? and *Where are* _____?
to ask about location.

A: <u>Where is</u> the bread?
B: It's on the counter.

B: <u>Where are</u> the plates?
A: They're on the table.

Ask and answer questions about where things
are in the kitchen.

A: Where _____?
B: _____.

25

 1. sofa
el sofá

 4. remote
el control remoto

 7. teléphone
el teléfono

 2. rug
la alfombra

 5. radio
el radio

 8. listen
escuchar

 3. television
el televisor

 6. music
la música

 9. talk
hablar

Describe Actions at Home

10. play
jugar

11. study
estudiar

12. help
ayudar

Use verbs with –*ing* to talk about what people are doing.

He's <u>listening</u> to music.
She's <u>studying</u>.
They're <u>playing</u> a game.

Talk about what people are doing in the living room.

He's _____ing on the phone.
She's _____ing _____.
He's _____ing _____.

27

9 Everyday Clothes
La ropa de todos los días

 1. dress
el vestido

 2. skirt
la falda

 3. pants
los pantalones

 4. jeans
los jeans

 5. T-shirt
la camiseta

 6. sweatshirt
la sudadera

 7. pajamas
el pijama

 8. underwear
la ropa interior

 9. socks
los calcetines

Determine Clothing Colors

10. cap
la gorra

11. shoes
los zapatos

12. sneakers
los tenis

Use *What color is _____?* and *What color are _____?* to ask about colors.

A: <u>What color is</u> the T-shirt?

B: It's purple.

B: <u>What color are</u> the jeans?

A: They're blue.

Ask and answer questions about colors.

A: What color _____?

B: _____.

29

Winter Holidays
el invierno

Rainy Spring
la primavera

 1. sweater
el suéter

 4. gloves
los guantes

 7. raincoat
el impermeable

 2. hat
el sombrero

 5. boots
las botas

 8. shorts
los pantalones cortos

 3. scarf
la bufanda

 6. umbrella
el paraguas

 9. sunglasses
los gafas de sol

Summer Vacation
el verano

Windy Fall
el otoño

10. bathing suit
el traje de baño

11. sandals
las sandalias

12. jacket
la chaqueta

Describe People's Clothes

 **Use the verb *wearing* to talk about people's clothes.**

He's <u>wearing</u> a raincoat.
She's <u>wearing</u> a sweater.
They're <u>wearing</u> hats.

Talk about the people in the pictures.

He's wearing _____.
She's wearing _____.
They're wearing _____.

A Read a Chart

Look at the Things at Home chart.

Things at Home		kitchen	living room	bedroom	bathroom
sofa			X		
sink		X			X
refrigerator		X			
bed				X	
window		X	X	X	X

B Discuss

Talk about the chart. Take turns.

There is a <u>sink</u> in the <u>bathroom</u>.
There is a <u>sofa</u> in the <u>living room</u>.
There is a <u>bed</u> and a _____ in the <u>bedroom</u>.
There is a _____ and a <u>refrigerator</u> in the _____.
There is a _____ in the _____.

C Make a Chart

Complete the chart in your notebook.

Things at Home				
	kitchen	living room	bedroom	bathroom
table				
dresser				
shower				
stove				
mirror				

D Discuss

👥 **Ask and answer questions about your chart. Take turns.**

A: Is there a <u>stove</u> in the <u>kitchen</u>?

B: Yes, there is a <u>stove</u> in the <u>kitchen</u>.

B: Is there a <u>table</u> in the <u>bathroom</u>?

A: No, there isn't a <u>table</u> in the <u>bathroom</u>.

A: Is there a _____ in the _____?

B: Yes, there is _____.

B: Is there a _____ in the _____?

A: No, there isn't _____.

E Think Critically

👥 **Talk with your class.**

List. Look at the charts.
1. How many rooms have a window? Name them.
2. How many things are in the kitchen? Name them.

Compare. Look at the charts.
1. Which things are in the bedroom and living room?
2. Pick two other rooms. Which things are in both rooms?

33

A Day at School
Un día en la escuela

1. read
leer

2. write
escribir

3. draw
dibujar

4. repeat
repetir

5. think
pensar

6. raise hand
levantar la mano

7. work with a partner
trabajar con un compañero

8. work in a group
trabajar en grupo

What is this?

9. ask questions
hacer preguntas

This is an apple.

10. answer questions
responder preguntas

Discuss School Activities

Use the verb *does* to ask questions about the students.

A: What <u>does</u> Alex do at school?
B: He reads.

B: What <u>does</u> Jasmine do at school?
A: She works in a group.

A: What <u>does</u> Tyler do at school?
B: He answers questions.

Ask and answer questions about the students at school.

A: What _____ Elena do at school?
B: She writes.

B: What does _____ do at school?
A: _____.

12 The School

La escuela

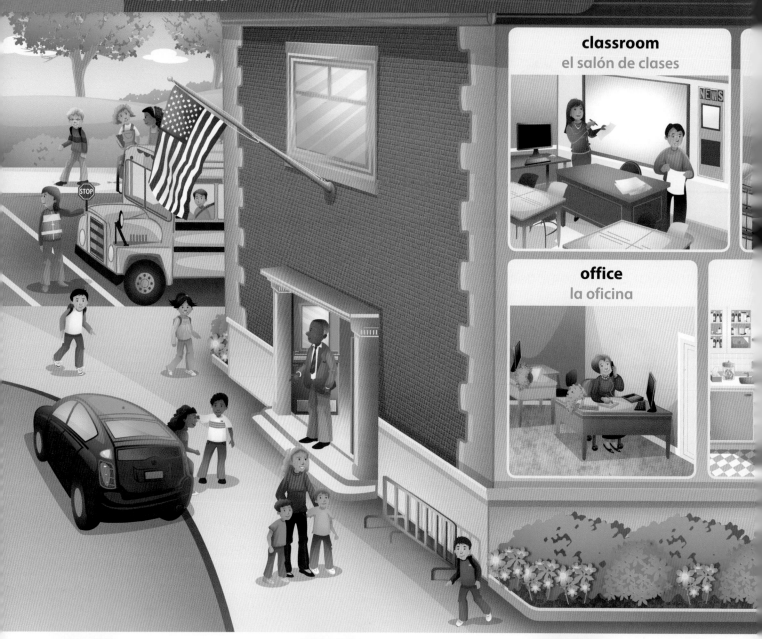

classroom
el salón de clases

office
la oficina

 1. crossing guard
el oficial de tránsito

 2. bus driver
el conductor de autobús

 3. student
el estudiante

 4. principal
el director

 5. teacher
la maestra

 6. teacher's aide
el ayudante

 7. librarian
la bibliotecaria

 8. secretary
la secretaria

 9. nurse
la enfermera

library
la biblioteca

computer room
el laboratorio de computación

art room
el salón de arteclases

music room
el salón de música

nurse's office
la enfermería

cafeteria
la cantinaclases

restroom
los baños

gym
el gimnasio

Locate People at School

10. cafeteria worker
la empleada de la cantina

11. custodian
el portero

12. coach
el entrenador

 Use *Where is* _____? to ask about people at school.

A: <u>Where is</u> the teacher?
B: She's in the classroom.

B: <u>Where is</u> the custodian?
A: He's in the restroom.

Ask and answer questions about where people are.

A: Where is the _____?
B: _____'s in the _____.

37

13 School Supplies
Los útiles escolares

 1. pencil
el lápiz

 2. colored pencil
el lápiz de color

 3. pencil sharpener
el sacapuntas

 **4.** eraser
la goma de borrar

 5. pen
la pluma

 6. crayon
el creyón

 7. marker
el marcador

 8. scissors
las tijeras

 9. calculator
la calculadora

Indicate Possession

10. book
el libro

11. binder
la carpeta

12. backpack
la mochila

Use *have* and *has* to talk about school supplies.

He <u>has</u> an eraser.

She <u>has</u> two pens.

They <u>have</u> colored pencils.

Talk about what the students have.

She has _____.

He has _____.

They have _____.

1. paper
el papel

2. notebook
el cuaderno

3. glue
el pegamento

4. tape
la cinta
adhesiva

5. ruler
la regla

6. chair
la silla

7. trash can
el bote de la
basura

8. board
la pizarra

9. clock
el reloj

Read your book.
Write your

Describe Location

10. globe
el globo terráqueo

11. map
el mapa

12. flag
la bandera

Use the prepositions *on* or *in* to talk about where things are.

The globe is <u>on</u> the desk.
The clock is <u>on</u> the wall.
The notebook is <u>in</u> the desk.
The paper is <u>in</u> the trash can.

Talk about where things are in the classroom.

The map is _____ the wall.
The paper is _____ the desk.
The _____ is _____ the _____.

41

1. catalog
el catálogo

2. call number
el código de
referencia

3. dictionary
el diccionario

4. atlas
el atlas

5. newspaper
el periódico

6. magazine
la revista

7. DVD
el DVD

8. bookshelves
las estanterías

9. library card
la tarjeta de la
biblioteca

Describe Actions at the Library

10. check out
sacar un libro

11. return
devolver un libro

12. look
mirar

Use verbs with *-ing* to talk about what someone is doing.

He's <u>checking</u> out a book.
She's <u>returning</u> a DVD.
They're <u>looking</u> at the catalog.

Talk about what the students are doing in the library.

He's _____ing _____.
She's _____ing _____.
They're _____ing _____.

 1. computer
la computadora

 2. monitor
el monitor

 3. keyboard
el teclado

 4. mouse
el mouse

 5. headphones
los auriculares

 6. microphone
el micrófono

 7. printer
la impresora

 8. Internet
la Internet

 9. cursor
el cursor

NO FOOD OR DRINK

Describe Actions in the Lab

10. log in
iniciar sesión

11. type
escribir

12. click
hacer clic

Talk about what students are doing in the computer lab with the verb *using*.

She's <u>using</u> a microphone.

He's <u>using</u> a mouse.

They're <u>using</u> computers.

Talk about what students are using in the computer lab.

He's using _____.

She's using _____.

They're using _____.

45

El almuerzo en la cantina

1. tray
la bandeja

4. carton
el envase

7. salad
la ensalada

2. bottle
la botella

5. can
la lata

8. strawberries
las fresas

3. bag
la bolsa

6. sandwich
el sándwich

9. carrots
las zanahorias

Describe Containers of Food

10. crackers
las galletas

11. juice
el jugo

12. milk
la leche

Use the preposition *of* to talk about food in the cafeteria.

She has a bag <u>of</u> carrots.

He has a can <u>of</u> juice.

She has a carton <u>of</u> milk.

Talk about lunch in the cafeteria.

She has a bag _____ crackers.

He has a bowl _____ strawberries.

She has a _____ of _____.

He has a _____ of _____.

47

1. field
el campo

4. balls
las pelotas

7. throw
lanzar

2. court
la cancha

5. jump
saltar

8. catch
atrapar

3. basket
la canasta

6. bounce
rebotar

9. kick
patear

Describe Physical Actions

	10. run correr
	11. fall caerse
	12. climb trepar

Use action verbs to talk about what people are doing.

He <u>throws</u> the ball.
She <u>kicks</u> the ball.
He <u>bounces</u> the ball on the court.

Talk about what the students are doing.

He _____ the ball.
She _____ on the field.
He _____.
She _____.

 1. earache
el dolor de oído

 4. cut
el corte

 7. tissues
los pañuelos de papel

 2. fever
la fiebre

 5. stomachache
el dolor de estómago

 8. bandage
la venda

 3. sore throat
el dolor de garganta

 6. thermometer
el termómetro

 9. bleed
sangrar

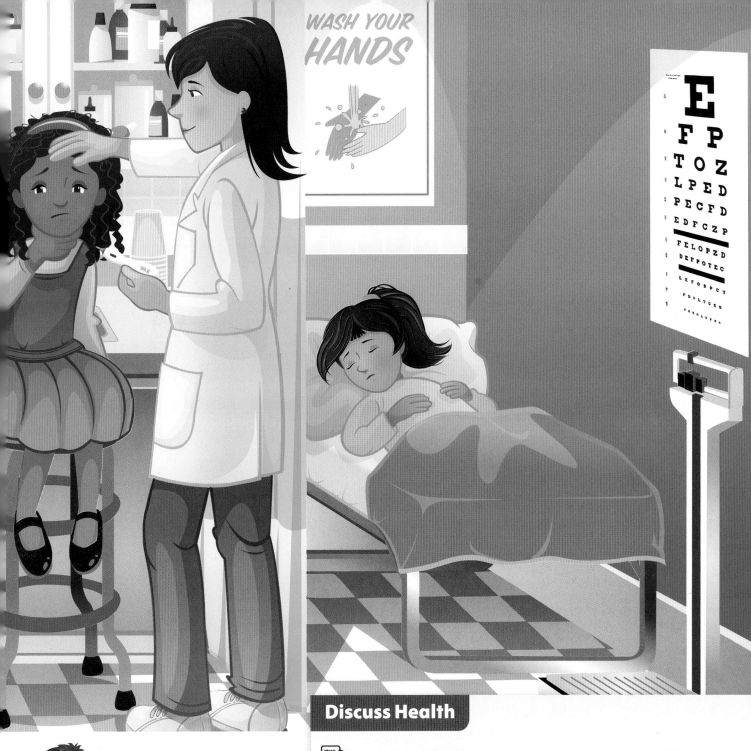

10. cough
toser

11. sneeze
estornudar

12. lie down
recostarse

Discuss Health

Use *What's the matter with _____?* to ask about someone's health.

A: <u>What's the matter with</u> him?
B: He has an earache.

B: <u>What's the matter with</u> her?
A: She's lying down.

Ask and answer questions about the students.

A: _____ with _____?
B: _____.

51

20 Feelings
Los sentimientos

 1. tired
cansado/a

 4. surprised
sorprendido/a

 7. confused
confundido/a

 2. sad
triste

 5. angry
enojado/a

 8. smile
sonreír

 3. happy
feliz

 6. scared
asustado/a

 9. frown
fruncir el ceño

10. yawn
bostezar

11. cry
llorar

12. laugh
reír

Describe Feelings

Use adjectives to talk about people's feelings.

Jasmine feels <u>angry</u>. She's frowning.
The boy feels <u>tired</u>. He's yawning.
The girl feels <u>happy</u>. She's smiling.

Talk about how the students feel.

Tyler feels _____. He's laughing.
Elena feels _____. She's frowning.
The boy feels _____. He's _____.
The girl feels _____. She's _____.

53

A Read a Diagram

Look at the Venn diagram.

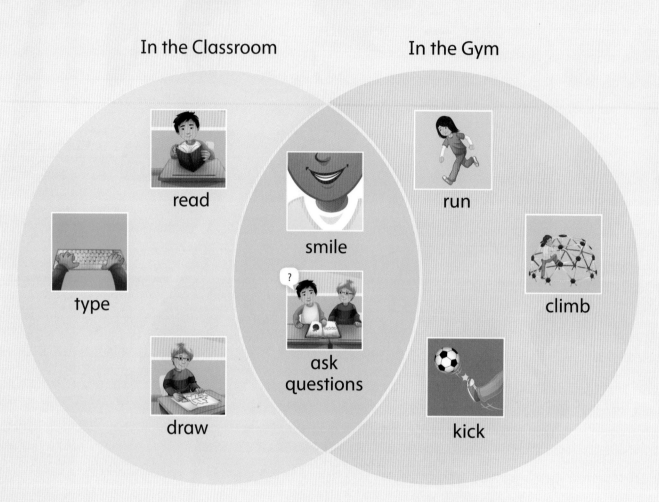

In the Classroom   In the Gym

read

smile

run

type

ask
questions

climb

draw

kick

B Discuss

Talk about the diagram. Take turns.

Students <u>read</u> in the classroom.

Students <u>run</u> in the gym.

Students <u>smile</u> in the classroom and the gym.

Students _____ in the _____.

Students _____ in the _____ and the _____.

C Make a Diagram

Complete the Venn diagram in your notebook.

Word Box

bounce

click

jump

laugh

log in

think

throw

write

In the Classroom   In the Gym

D Discuss

Ask and answer questions about your diagram. Take turns.

A: Do students <u>jump</u> in the gym?

B: Yes, they <u>jump</u> in the gym.

B: Do students <u>write</u> in the gym?

A: No, they don't <u>write</u> in the gym.

A: Do students think in the _____?

B: Yes, _____.

B: Do students _____?

A: _____, they _____.

E Think Critically

Talk with your class.

List. Look at the diagrams.

1. What do students do in the classroom?

2. What do students do in the classroom and the gym?

Make Connections. Look at the diagrams.

1. What do you do in the classroom? In the gym?

2. What else do you do at school?

21 People at Work

La gente en el trabajo

1. build houses
construir casas

2. fix cars
reparar coches

3. sell clothing
vender ropa

4. deliver mail
entregar el correo

5. serve food
servir alimentos

6. take care of people
cuidar a las personas

7. protect the community
proteger a la comunidad

8. fight fires
combatir incendios

9. grow crops
cultivar

10. raise animals
criar animales

Discuss People at Work

Use **verbs** to ask and answer questions about what people do at work.

A: What does he <u>build</u>?
B: He <u>builds</u> houses.

B: What does she <u>protect</u>?
A: She <u>protects</u> the community.

A: What does she <u>fix</u>?
B: She <u>fixes</u> cars.

Ask and answer questions about what people do at work.

A: Who does he take care of?
B: He takes care of _____.

B: What does she grow?
A: She _____ crops.

A: What does he _____?
B: He _____.

B: What does she _____?
A: She _____.

22 | The Neighborhood
El vecindario

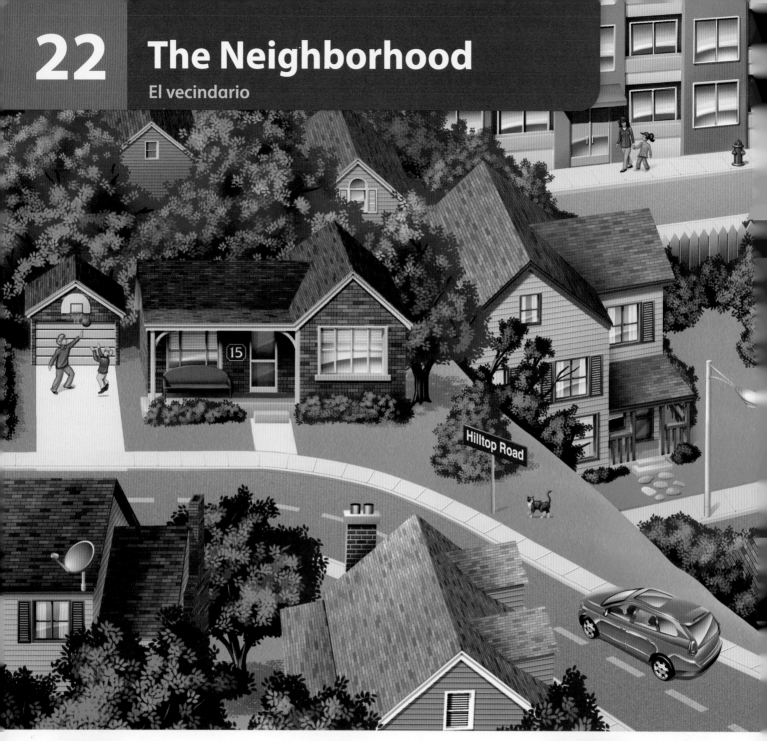

	1. house la casa		**4.** street sign el letrero
			**5.** address el la dirección
	2. apartment building el edificio de apartamentos		
	3. street la calle		**6.** sidewalk la acera

	7. corner la esquina
	8. streetlight la luz de la calle
	9. stop sign la señal de alto

Describe Location

10. fence
el cerco

11. park
el parque

12. bench
la banca

Use *There's* _____. to talk about places in the neighborhood.

<u>There's</u> a red house on Oak Street.

<u>There's</u> a street sign on the corner.

<u>There's</u> a bench in the park.

Talk about places in the neighborhood.

There's a _____ on the sidewalk.

There's a _____ on Maple Street.

There's _____.

59

23 The Community
La comunidad

 1. police officer
el oficial de policía

 2. mail carrier
la cartera

 3. post office
la oficina de correos

 4. police station
la estación de policía

 5. movie theater
el cine

 6. museum
el museo

 7. intersection
la intersección

 8. crosswalk
el cruce peatonal

 9. traffic light
el semáforo

60 Unit 3 Community

COMMUNITY THEATER
SHOWTIMES
THURS-SAT 8PM SAT-SUN 2PM

COMING SOON!

TURTLES

TURTLES

ART MUSEUM

TAXI

POST OFFICE

PUBLIC LIBRARY

MAIL

MAIL

MAIL

Discuss Location

10. mailbox
el buzón

11. taxi
el taxi

12. cross the street
cruzar la calle

Use the preposition *next to* to answer questions about where things are.

A: Where's the police station?

B: It's <u>next to</u> the movie theater.

Ask and answer questions about where things are in the community.

A: Where's the movie theater?

B: It's _____ the museum.

B: Where's the _____?

A: It's _____.

61

SUPER SHOES

PHARMACY

OXFORD MARKET

 1. cashier
la cajera

 4. teller
el cajero del banco

 7. drugstore
la farmacia

 2. pharmacist
la farmacéutica

 5. customer
el cliente

 8. shoe store
la zapatería

 3. salesperson
el vendedor

 6. supermarket
el supermercado

 9. bank
el banco

LAUNDRY

GAS

GAS

OXFORD MARKET

BANK

SALE

SALE

Discuss Where People Work

10. gas station
la gasolinera

11. laundry
la lavandería

12. groceries
los abarrotes

Use *Where does* _____ *work?* to ask about people and their jobs.

A: <u>Where does</u> a teller <u>work</u>?

B: A teller works at a bank.

Ask and answer questions about where people work.

A: Where does a pharmacist _____?

B: A _____ works at a _____.

B: Where does a _____ work?

A: A _____ works at a _____.

63

The Supermarket
El supermercado

SEAFOOD

MEAT

 1. celery
el apio

 2. lettuce
la lechuga

 3. tomato
el tomate

 4. avocado
el aguacate

 5. apple
la manzana

 6. pineapple
la piña

 7. orange
la naranja

 8. lemon
el limón

 9. list
la lista

Describe Future Actions

10. paper towels
las toallas de papel

11. box
la caja

12. cart
el carrito

Use *going to* to talk about the future.

She's <u>going to</u> buy a lemon.

He's <u>going to</u> buy apples.

They're <u>going to</u> buy paper towels.

Talk about what people are going to buy.

He's _____ buy _____.

She's _____ buy _____.

They're _____ buy _____.

65

26 The Restaurant
El restaurante

 1. menu
el menú

 4. chicken
el pollo

 7. fork
el tenedor

 2. server
el mesero

 5. rice
el arroz

 8. spoon
la cuchara

 3. soup
la sopa

 6. broccoli
el brócoli

 9. knife
el cuchillo

Identify What People Need

10. napkin
la servilleta

11. bowl
el tazón

12. order
pedir

Use the verb *need* to talk about things that people are missing.

She <u>needs</u> a napkin.

He <u>needs</u> a spoon.

She <u>needs</u> rice.

Talk about what people need at the restaurant.

He _____ a bowl.

She _____ a menu.

He needs _____.

She needs _____.

1. bicycle
la bicicleta

2. car
el coche

3. bus
el autobús

4. bus stop
la parada de autobús

5. seat belt
el cinturón de seguridad

6. helmet
el casco

7. building
el edificio

8. garden
el jardín

9. wait
esperar

Describe Transportation

10. walk
caminar

11. ride
andar

12. drive
conducir

Use verbs to talk about getting around the city.

He <u>drives</u> a bus.
She <u>waits</u> for the bus.
They <u>ride</u> bicycles.

Talk about getting around the city.

She _____ a car.
He _____ the bus.
She _____.
He _____.
They _____.

 1. motorcycle
la motocicleta

 4. police car
la patrulla de
policía

 7. helicopter
el helicóptero

 2. truck
el camión

 5. train
el tren

 8. airport
el aeropuerto

 3. van
la camioneta

 6. airplane
el avión

 9. highway
la carretera

Describe Distance

 Use the prepositions *near* and *far from* to talk about distance.

The helicopter is <u>near</u> the airport.
The factory is <u>far from</u> the train.
The truck is <u>near</u> the motorcycle.

Talk about the city.

The _____ is far from the airplane.
The _____ is near the _____.
The _____ is far from the _____.

 10. sign
el señal

 11. factory
la fábrica

 12. skyscraper
el rascacielos

29 The Harbor
El puerto

 1. sailboat
el velero

 2. ship
el barco

 3. ferry
el ferry

 4. tugboat
el remolcador

 5. boats
los botes

 6. lighthouse
el faro

 7. bridge
el puente

 8. dock
el muelle

 9. crane
la grúa

Identify Quantity

10. life jacket
el chaleco
salvavidas

11. load
cargar

12. unload
descargar

Use *How many* _____? **to ask about the harbor.**

A: How many cranes are on the dock?

B: One crane is on the dock.

B: How many cars are on the bridge?

A: Five cars are on the bridge.

Ask and answer questions about the harbor.

A: How many _____ are _____?

B: _____.

73

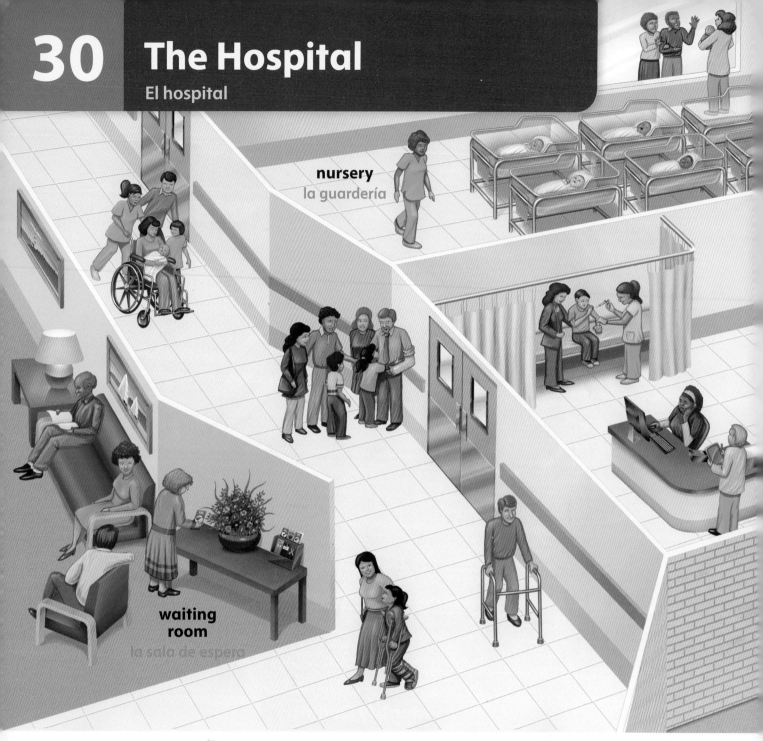

30 The Hospital
El hospital

nursery
la guardería

waiting
room
la sala de espera

 1. wheelchair
la silla de ruedas

 4. shot
la inyección

 7. paramedic
el paramédico

 2. crutches
las muletas

 5. X-ray
la radiografía

 8. patient
el paciente

 3. cast
el yeso

 6. ambulance
la ambulancia

 9. receptionist
la recepcionista

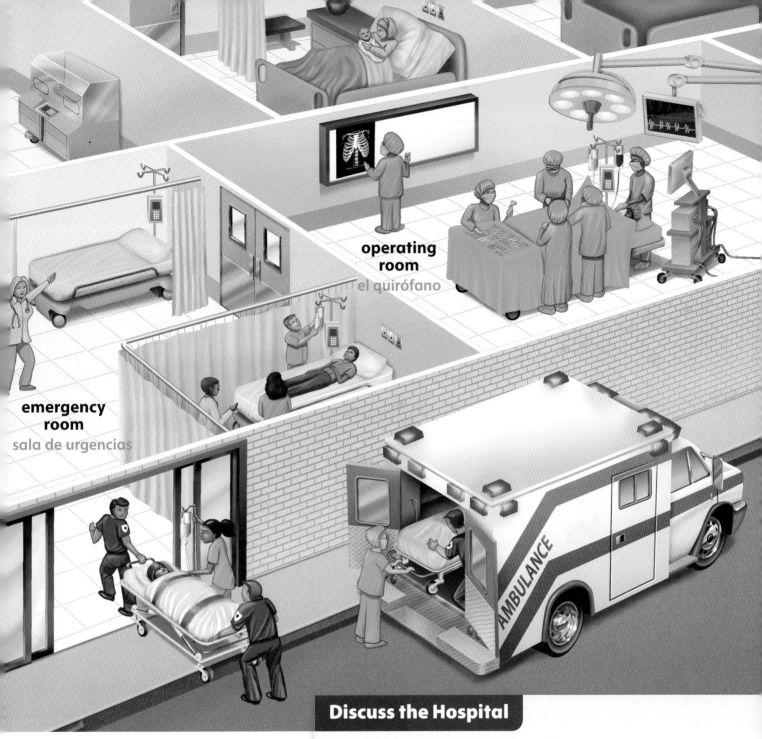

operating room
el quirófano

emergency room
sala de urgencias

AMBULANCE

Discuss the Hospital

10. doctor
la doctora

11. surgeon
el cirujano

12. baby
el bebé

Use *Who* _____? to ask about people in the hospital.

A: <u>Who</u> is in the emergency room?
B: The receptionist is in the emergency room.

B: <u>Who</u> is in the ambulance?
A: The paramedic is in the ambulance.

Ask and answer questions about people in the hospital.

A: Who is in the _____?
B: The _____ is in the _____.

75

31 Fire Safety
Prevención de incendios

1. firefighter
el bombero

4. matches
los cerillos

7. battery
la batería

2. uniform
el uniforme

5. smoke
el humo

8. fire extinguisher
el extinguidor de incendios

3. fire truck
el camión de bomberos

6. smoke detector
el detector de humo

9. fire escape
la escalera de emergencia

Don't play with matches!

Does your smoke detector need a battery?

Plan your escape route.

Call 911 for help!

911

Discuss Fire Safety

10. escape route
la vía de evacuación

11. exit
la salida

12. call 911
llamar al 911

 Use **commands** to talk about fire safety.

<u>Know</u> the exits.
<u>Find</u> the fire escape.
<u>Make</u> sure the smoke detector has a battery.

Talk about fire safety.

Don't play with _____.
Call _____ for help.
Plan your escape _____.
Use the _____.

 1. farmer
el granjero

 4. orchard
la huerta

 7. chicken
el pollo

 2. barn
el granero

 5. field
el campo

 8. cow
la vaca

 3. tractor
el tractor

 6. crops
los cultivos

 9. horse
el caballo

Describe the Farm

10. plow
arar

11. feed
alimentar

12. pick
recoger

 Use verbs to talk about the farm.

She <u>feeds</u> chickens.
The farmer <u>plows</u> the field.
They <u>pick</u> apples in the orchard.

Talk about the farm.

He _____ apples.
She _____ horses in the barn.
They grow crops in the _____.

79

A Read a Chart

Look at the People and Places chart.

People Who Work →		Places to Work	
police officer		police station	
cashier		supermarket	
mail carrier		post office	
receptionist		hospital	
teller		bank	

B Discuss

Talk about the chart. Take turns.

A <u>police officer</u> works at a <u>police station</u>.

A <u>cashier</u> works at a _____.

A _____ works at a <u>hospital</u>.

A _____ works at a _____.

C Make a Chart

Complete the chart in your notebook.

Word Box

doctor

drugstore

farm

farmer

hospital

pharmacist

restaurant

salesperson

server

shoe store

People Who Work →	Places to Work

D Discuss

Ask and answer questions about your chart. Take turns.

A: Who works at a <u>restaurant</u>?

B: A <u>server</u> works at a <u>restaurant</u>.

B: Who works at a <u>drugstore</u>?

A: A _____ works at a <u>drugstore</u>.

A: Who works at a <u>shoe store</u>?

B: A _____ works at a _____.

B: Who works at a _____?

A: A _____ works at a _____.

E Think Critically

Talk with your class.

Make Connections. Look at the chart in A.

1. Where does a cashier work?

2. Where else does a cashier work?

Evaluate. Look at both charts.

1. Where do you want to work?

2. Why do you want to work there?

1. be born
nacer

2. die
morir

3. explore
explorar

4. trade
comerciar

5. sign a document
firmar un documento

6. travel
viajar

7. invent
inventar

8. immigrate
inmigrar

9. celebrate
celebrar

Discuss the Past

 Use verbs with -ed to talk about the past.

He <u>signed</u> a document in 1776.
She <u>traveled</u> in 1867.
They <u>immigrated</u> in 1920.
They <u>traded</u> in 1770.

Talk about the past.

He explored in _____.
She died in _____.
They celebrated in _____.
He _____ in _____.
She _____ in _____.
They _____ in _____.

83

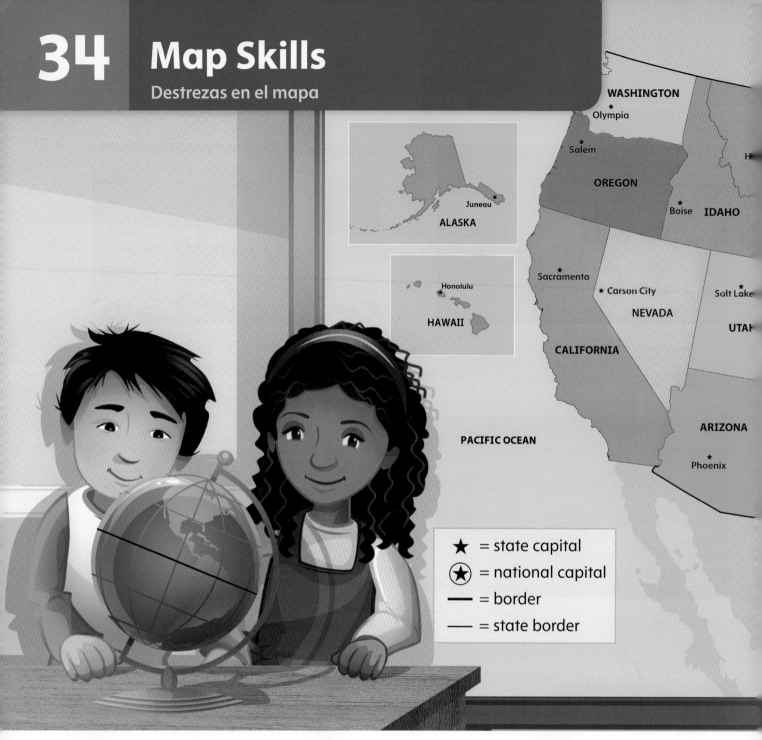

WASHINGTON
★ Olympia

★ Salem

OREGON

Boise ★ IDAHO

ALASKA
Juneau ★

HAWAII
Honolulu

Sacramento ★

★ Carson City

Salt Lake

NEVADA

UTAH

CALIFORNIA

PACIFIC OCEAN

ARIZONA

Phoenix ★

★ = state capital
⊛ = national capital
— = border
— = state border

 1. ocean
el océano

 4. state
el estado

 7. equator
el ecuador

 2. continent
el continente

 5. capital
la capital

 8. hemisphere
el hemisferio

 3. country
el país

 6. border
la frontera

★ = state capital
⊛ = national capital
█ = border
— = state border
9. key
la clave

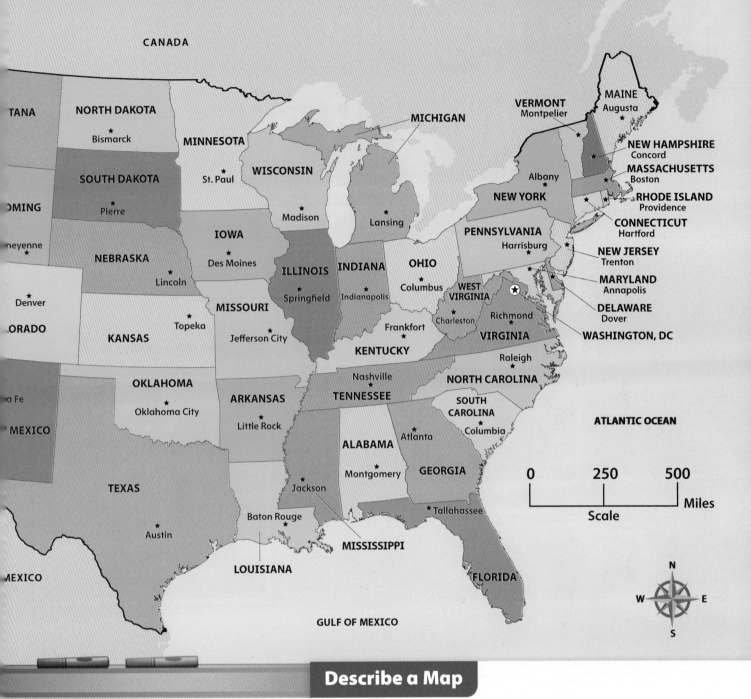

CANADA

MONTANA

NORTH DAKOTA
★ Bismarck

MINNESOTA
★ St. Paul

WISCONSIN
★ Madison

MICHIGAN
★ Lansing

VERMONT
Montpelier

MAINE
Augusta ★

NEW HAMPSHIRE
Concord

MASSACHUSETTS
★ Boston

SOUTH DAKOTA
★ Pierre

WYOMING
Cheyenne ★

NEBRASKA
★ Lincoln

IOWA
★ Des Moines

ILLINOIS
★ Springfield

INDIANA
★ Indianapolis

OHIO
★ Columbus

NEW YORK
Albany ★

RHODE ISLAND
Providence

CONNECTICUT
Hartford

Denver ★
COLORADO

KANSAS
★ Topeka

MISSOURI
★ Jefferson City

KENTUCKY
★ Frankfort

WEST
VIRGINIA
★ Charleston

PENNSYLVANIA
Harrisburg ★

NEW JERSEY
Trenton

MARYLAND
Annapolis

DELAWARE
Dover

WASHINGTON, DC

VIRGINIA
Richmond ★

Santa Fe

OKLAHOMA
★ Oklahoma City

ARKANSAS
★ Little Rock

TENNESSEE
Nashville ★

NORTH CAROLINA
Raleigh ★

NEW MEXICO

ALABAMA
★ Montgomery

SOUTH
CAROLINA
Columbia ★

ATLANTIC OCEAN

TEXAS
★ Austin

Jackson ★

Atlanta ★

GEORGIA

Tallahassee ★

MEXICO

Baton Rouge

MISSISSIPPI

LOUISIANA

FLORIDA

GULF OF MEXICO

```
0        250      500
|----|----|----|----| Miles
        Scale
```

N
W   E
S

Describe a Map

10. symbols
los símbolos

11. scale
la escala

12. compass rose
la rosa de los vientos

✍ **Use the verb *shows* to talk about a map.**

The color blue <u>shows</u> the ocean.

The black line <u>shows</u> the border.

The key <u>shows</u> symbols.

👥 **Talk about the map.**

The star _____ the capital.

The _____ shows the equator.

The _____ shows _____.

85

LEADERS

Country

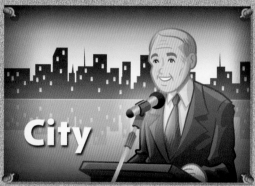

City

State

1. president
el presidente

4. judge
la jueza

7. leaders
los líderes

2. governor
la gobernadora

5. city council
el ayuntamiento

8. citizen
el ciudadano

3. mayor
el alcalde

6. council member
el miembro del
ayuntamiento

9. courtroom
la sala de un
tribunal

City Council Meeting

Court

Election

VOTE HERE

10. speech
el discurso

11. ballot
la boleta
electoral

12. vote
votar

Discuss Leaders

 Use *Who leads* _____? to ask questions about the government.

A: <u>Who leads</u> the city?

B: The mayor leads the city.

B: <u>Who leads</u> the country?

A: The president leads the country.

 Ask and answer questions about the government.

A: Who leads the _____?

B: The _____ leads the _____.

87

36 American Symbols

Los símbolos de los Estados Unidos

Washington Monument

Pledge of Allegiance
by Francis Bellamy

I pledge allegiance
to the flag
of the United States
of America,
and to the republic
for which it stands,
one nation under God,
indivisible,
with liberty
and justice for all.

1. Statue of Liberty
la Estatua de la Libertad

2. White House
la Casa Blanca

3. Capitol
el Capitolio

4. Congress
el Congreso

5. Supreme Court
la Corte Suprema

6. monument
el monumento

7. memorial
el monumento conmemorativo

8. eagle
el águila

9. Pledge of Allegiance
el Juramento de Lealtad

The Star Spangled Banner
by Francis Scott Key
on September 14th, 1814

O! say can you see by the dawn's early light,
What so proudly we hailed at the twilight's last gleaming,
Whose broad stripes and bright stars through the perilous fight,
O'er the ramparts we watched, were so gallantly streaming?
And the rockets' red glare, the bombs bursting in air,
Gave proof through the night that our flag was still there;
O! say does that star-spangled banner yet wave,
O'er the land of the free and the home of the brave?

New York

Lincoln Memorial

Discuss American Symbols

10. national anthem
el himno nacional

11. stars
las estrellas

12. stripes
las rayas

📝 Use *What is* _____? **to ask questions about American symbols.**

A: <u>What is</u> the bald eagle?
B: It's an American symbol.

B: <u>What is</u> "The Star-Spangled Banner"?
A: It's the national anthem.

👥 **Ask and answer questions about American symbols.**

A: What is _____?
B: It's _____.

89

A Read a Chart

Look at The United States chart.

The United States

	country	state	city
national anthem The Star Spangled Banner by Francis Scott Key September 14th, 1814 O! say can you see by the dawn's early light,	X		
governor		X	
monument	X	X	X
city council			X
Supreme Court	X		

B Discuss

Talk about the chart. Take turns.

The state has a <u>governor</u>.
The country has a <u>national anthem</u>.
The city has a <u>monument</u> and a _____.
The country has a _____ and a <u>Supreme Court</u>.
The _____ has a _____.

C Make a Chart

Complete the chart in your notebook.

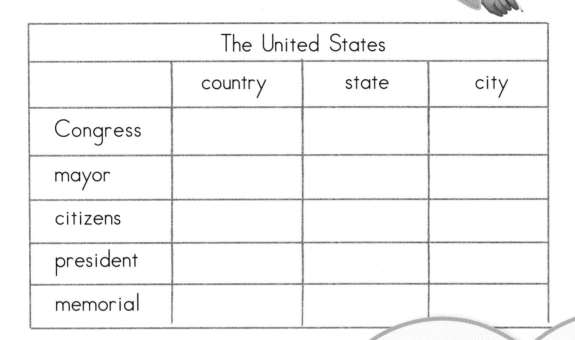

The United States			
	country	state	city
Congress			
mayor			
citizens			
president			
memorial			

D Discuss

Ask and answer questions about your chart. Take turns.

A: Does the city have <u>citizens</u>?

B: Yes, it has <u>citizens</u>.

B: Does the state have a <u>mayor</u>?

A: No, it doesn't have a <u>mayor</u>.

A: Does the _____ have _____?

B: Yes, it has _____.

B: Does the _____ have _____?

A: No, it doesn't have _____.

E Think Critically

Talk with your class.

List. Look at the charts.

1. What people and things does the country have?

2. What people and things does the city have?

Compare. Look at the charts.

1. How are the country, state, and city the same?

2. How are they different?

Healthy Habits

Hábitos saludables

1. wash hands
lavarse las manos

2. exercise
hacer ejercicio

3. drink water
beber agua

4. sleep
dormir

5. floss
limpiarse los dientes con hilo dental

6. go to the dentist
ir a la dentista

7. get a checkup
hacerse un chequeo

8. cover mouth
cubrirse la boca al toser

9. use a tissue
usar pañuelos de papel

10. wear sunblock
usar protector solar

Describe Frequency

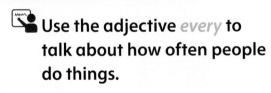 **Use the adjective *every* to talk about how often people do things.**

Elena flosses <u>every</u> day.
She gets a checkup <u>every</u> year.
She drinks water <u>every</u> day.
She uses a tissue <u>every</u> time
  she sneezes.

Talk about Elena's healthy habits.

Elena sleeps _____ day.
She covers her mouth _____
  time she coughs.
She exercises _____.
She _____ every day.
She _____ every year.
She _____ every _____.

93

Smiling Faces!

 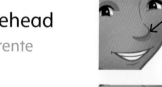

1. forehead
la frente

4. nose
la nariz

7. tongue
la lengua

2. eyebrow
la ceja

5. mouth
la boca

8. lips
los labios

3. eyelid
el párpado

6. gums
las encías

9. teeth
los dientes

Silly Faces

Describe Faces

10. cheek
la mejilla

11. chin
la barbilla

12. ear
la oreja

Use the prepositions *above* and *below* to talk about faces.

The nose is <u>above</u> the mouth.
The chin is <u>below</u> the forehead.
The eyebrows are <u>above</u> the eyes.

Talk about faces.

The chin is _____ the nose.
The eyes are _____ the mouth.
The _____ is above the _____.
The _____ is below the _____.

95

39 Parts of Body
Las partes del cuerpo

 1. head
la cabeza

 2. neck
el cuello

 3. shoulder
el hombro

 4. chest
el pecho

 5. back
la espalda

 6. leg
la pierna

 7. knee
la rodilla

 8. foot
el pie

 9. ankle
el tobillo

96   **Unit 5** Health

Describe Parts of the Body

10. arm
el brazo

11. hand
la mano

12. wrist
la muñeca

Use the preposition *between* **to talk about the parts of the body.**

The wrist is <u>between</u> the hand and the arm.

The neck is <u>between</u> the head and the shoulders.

Talk about the parts of the body.

The _____ is between the foot and the leg.

The _____ is between the shoulders.

The _____ is between the _____.

97

1. brain
el cerebro

 4. stomach
el estómago

 7. ribs
las costillas

 2. heart
el corazón

 5. muscle
el músculo

 8. skin
la piel

 3. lungs
los pulmones

 6. bone
el hueso

 9. finger
el dedo de la mano

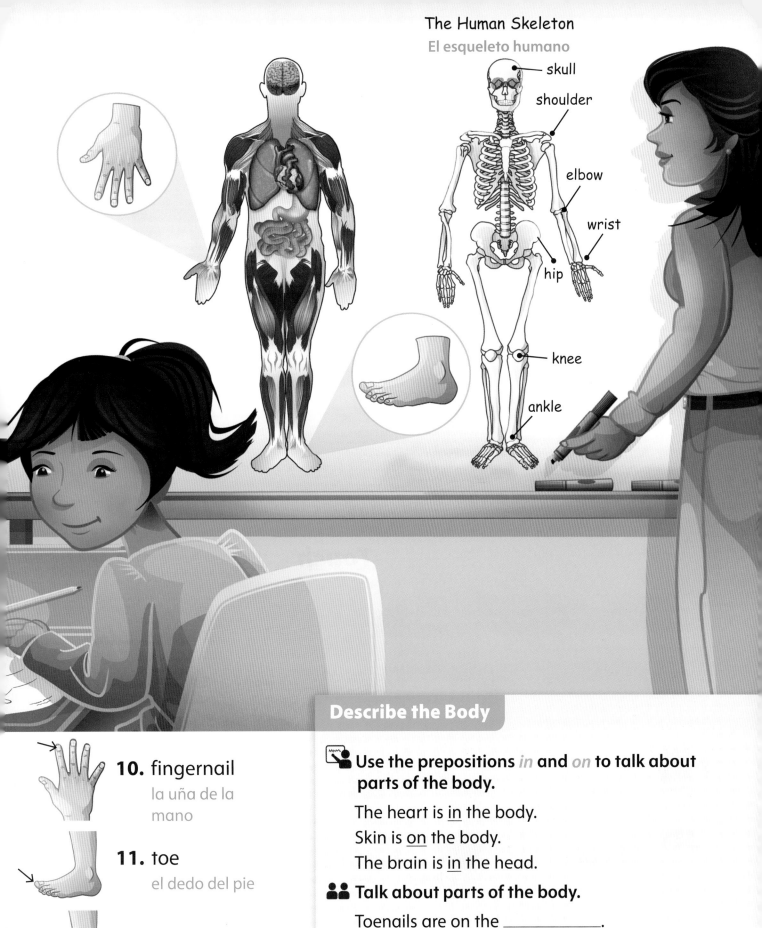

The Human Skeleton
El esqueleto humano

- skull
- shoulder
- elbow
- wrist
- hip
- knee
- ankle

10. fingernail
la uña de la mano

11. toe
el dedo del pie

12. toenail
la uña del pie

Describe the Body

Use the prepositions *in* and *on* to talk about parts of the body.

The heart is <u>in</u> the body.
Skin is <u>on</u> the body.
The brain is <u>in</u> the head.

Talk about parts of the body.

Toenails are on the _____.
_____ are in the body.
_____ is on the _____.
_____ is in the _____.

Sight
la vista

Touch
el tacto

 1. see
ver

 4. feel
sentir

 7. rough
áspero/a

 2. hear
oír

 5. smell
oler

 8. smooth
suave

 3. taste
saborear

 6. shiny
brillante

 9. sweet
dulce

Taste
el gusto

Quiet Please!

Hearing
el oído

Smell
el olfato

Describe Senses

10. sour
agrio/a

11. loud
ruidoso/a

12. quiet
silencioso/a

 Use adjectives to talk about people and senses.

She feels the <u>rough</u> rock.

He sees the <u>shiny</u> penny.

Talk about people and senses.

She feels _____.

He hears _____.

She sees _____.

He smells _____.

She tastes _____.

 1. oatmeal
la avena

 2. pasta
la pasta

 3. spinach
la espinaca

 4. peppers
los pimientos

 5. sweet potato
el camote

 6. corn
el maíz

 7. peach
el durazno

 8. pear
la pera

 9. yogurt
el yogur

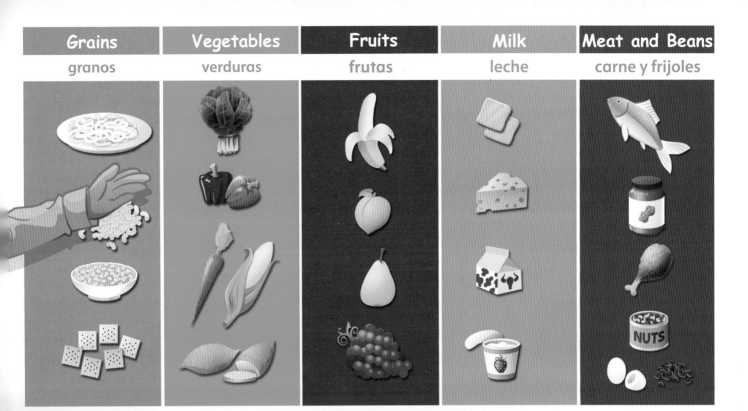

Grains	Vegetables	Fruits	Milk	Meat and Beans
granos	verduras	frutas	leche	carne y frijoles

Describe Food Groups

10. cheese
el queso

11. nuts
los frutos secos

12. fish
el pescado

 Use *part of* **to talk about food groups.**

A peach is <u>part of</u> the fruit group.
Pasta is <u>part of</u> the grain group.
Peppers are <u>part of</u> the vegetable group.
Nuts are <u>part of</u> the meat and bean group.

Talk about food groups.

Cheese is _____ the milk group.
_____ is part of the _____ group.
_____ are part of the _____ group.

103

A Read a Chart

Look at the Parts of the Body chart.

Parts of the Body

one	two	many
head	eyebrows	toes
neck	lips	fingernails
heart	lungs	bone

B Discuss

Talk about the chart. Take turns.

I have one <u>head</u>.

I have two <u>eyebrows</u>.

I have many _____.

I have _____.

Make a Chart

Complete the chart in your notebook.

Word Box	Parts of the Body		
back	**one**	**two**	**many**
brain			
ears			
knees			
muscles			
shoulders			
stomach			
teeth			
toenails			

D **Discuss**

👥 **Ask and answer questions about your chart. Take turns.**

A: Do you have many <u>teeth</u>?

B: Yes, I have many <u>teeth</u>.

B: Do you have two <u>brains</u>?

A: No, I have one _____.

A: Do you have _____?

B: Yes, I have _____.

B: Do you have _____?

A: No, I have _____.

E **Think Critically**

👥 **Talk with your class.**

List. Look at the charts.

1. Name the body parts you have one of.

2. Name the body parts you have two of.

Infer. Look at the charts.

1. Do you have the same number of teeth and bones?

2. Is *many* a number you can count? Why or why not?

1. observe
observar

2. magnifying glass
la lupa

3. microscope
el microscopio

4. binoculars
los binoculares

5. measure
medir

6. ruler
la regla

7. meter stick
la regla de un metro

8. measuring tape
la cinta métrica

9. measuring cup
la taza de medir

10. thermometer
el termómetro

Discuss Science Processes

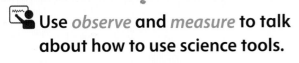 Use *observe* and *measure* to talk about how to use science tools.

Use a magnifying glass to <u>observe</u>.
Use a meter stick to <u>measure</u>.
Use binoculars to <u>observe</u>.
Use a measuring cup to <u>measure</u>.

Talk about science tools.

Use a measuring tape to _____.
Use a microscope to _____.
Use a _____ to measure.
Use a _____ to observe.
Use a _____ to _____.

 1. flowers
las flores

 4. stem
el tallo

 7. roots
las raíces

 2. petal
el pétalo

 5. thorn
la espina

 8. seeds
las semillas

 3. bud
el capullo

 6. leaf
la hoja

 9. seedling
la planta de semillero

Describe Plants

10. bulb
el bulbo

11. pollen
el polen

12. bee
la abeja

Use the adjectives *small* and *large* to talk about plants.

The tulip has <u>large</u> flowers.
The seedling has <u>small</u> roots.
The iris has <u>large</u> leaves.

Talk about the plants.

The rose has _____ thorns.
The _____ has _____ petals.
The _____ has _____.

bison
el bisonte

kangaroo
el canguro

tiger
el tigre

 1. beak
el pico

 4. fur
la piel

 7. tail
la cola

 2. wing
el ala

 5. paw
la pata

 8. whiskers
los bigotes

 3. feather
la pluma

 6. claw
la garra

 9. pouch
la bolsa

antelope
el antílope

monkey

gorilla
el gorila

Discuss Animals

10. antlers
el cuerno

11. hoof
la pezuña

12. shell
el caparazón

Use *Which* _____? to ask about animals.

A: Which animal has antlers?
B: The antelope has antlers.

B: Which animal has a tail?
A: The tiger has a tail.

Ask and answer questions about the animals.

A: Which animal has _____?
B: The _____ has _____.

111

 1. cocoon
el capullo

 4. tadpole
el renacuajo

 7. cat
el gato

 2. caterpillar
la oruga

 5. frog
la rana

 8. nest
el nido

 3. butterfly
la mariposa

 6. kitten
el gatito

 9. egg
el huevo

Describe Change

10. chick
el pollito

11. bird
el pájaro

12. hatch
salir del cascarón

Use the verb *becomes* to talk about how animals change.

The chick <u>becomes</u> a bird.
The tadpole <u>becomes</u> a frog.
The caterpillar <u>becomes</u> a butterfly.

Talk about how the animals change.

The kitten becomes a _____.
The cocoon becomes a _____.
The _____ becomes a _____.

1. seaweed
el alga marina

2. coral
el coral

3. shark
el tiburón

4. dolphin
el delfín

5. octopus
el pulpo

6. ray
la raya

7. crab
el cangrejo

8. fin
la aleta

9. gills
las branquias

Describe Ocean Animals

10. scales
las escamas

11. blowhole
el orificio para
respirar

12. tentacles
los tentáculos

Use the verb *has* to talk about animals and their body parts.

A dolphin <u>has</u> a blowhole.
A fish <u>has</u> scales.
An octopus <u>has</u> tentacles.

Talk about the animals.

A ray _____ gills.
A shark has _____.
A _____ has _____.

115

1. snake
la serpiente

4. hawk
el halcón

7. rabbit
el conejo

2. lizard
el lagarto

5. coyote
el coyote

8. mouse
el ratón

3. scorpion
el escorpión

6. prairie dog
el perro de las
praderas

9. cactus
el cactus

Discuss Animal Behavior

10. sand
la arena

11. dunes
las dunas

12. hole
la madriguera

Use *hides in* and *hides under* to talk about animals in the desert.

The bird <u>hides in</u> the cactus.
The scorpion <u>hides under</u> a rock.
The prairie dog <u>hides in</u> a hole.

Talk about where the animals hide.

The snake _____ a rock.
The mouse hides _____.
The _____ hides under _____.
The _____ hides in _____.

117

49 The Forest

El bosque

1. pine tree
el pino

2. oak tree
el roble

3. trunk
el tronco

4. bark
la corteza

5. pine cone
la piña

6. needles
las agujas

7. acorn
la bellota

8. bear
el oso

9. deer
el ciervo

Discuss Similarities

10. squirrel
la ardilla

11. woodpecker
el pájaro
carpintero

12. mosquito
el mosquito

Use the adverb *too* to talk about how things are the same.

A pine tree has a trunk.
An oak tree has a trunk <u>too</u>.

A deer has fur.
A bear has fur <u>too</u>.

Talk about the forest.

A _____ has _____.
A _____ has _____ too.

1. turtle
la tortuga

4. owl
el búho

7. moth
la polilla

2. jaguar
el jaguar

5. parrot
el loro

8. spider
la araña

3. bat
el murciélago

6. dragonfly
la libélula

9. ant
la hormiga

10. orchid
la orquídea

11. fern
el helecho

12. moss
el musgo

Describe Movement

Use the verbs *walks* and *flies* to talk about how animals move.

A jaguar <u>walks</u>.
A moth <u>flies</u>.
A turtle <u>walks</u>.

Talk about how the animals move.

An owl _____.
A _____ walks.
A _____ flies.

121

1. watering hole
el abrevadero

4. lion
el león

7. hippopotamus
el hipopótamo

2. grass
el pasto

5. hyena
la hiena

8. zebra
la cebra

3. flamingo
el flamenco

6. leopard
el leopardo

9. elephant
el elefante

Determine Distance

10. giraffe
la jirafa

11. spots
las manchas

12. stripes
las rayas

Use the prepositions *near* and *far from* to talk about the animals.

The leopard is <u>far from</u> the giraffes.

The hippopotamus is <u>near</u> the zebras.

The lion is <u>far from</u> the watering hole.

Talk about the animals.

The flamingo is far from _____.

The _____ is near the trees.

The _____ is far from _____.

The _____ is near _____.

123

A **Read a Chart**

Look at the Animal Features chart.

Animal Features		tail	wings	fin	paws
fish		X		X	
snake		X			
squirrel		X			X
parrot		X	X		
lion		X			X

B **Discuss**

👥 **Talk about the chart. Take turns.**

A <u>parrot</u> has <u>wings</u>.

A <u>snake</u> has a <u>tail</u>.

A <u>lion</u> has a <u>tail</u> and _____.

A _____ has a <u>tail</u> and a <u>fin</u>.

A _____ has _____.

C Make a Chart

Complete the chart in your notebook.

Animal Features			
	feathers	scales	fur
fish ✓		✓	✗
snake ✓		✓	
squirrel ✓			✓
parrot	✓		
lion			✓

D Discuss

Ask and answer questions about your chart. Take turns.

A: Does a <u>parrot</u> have <u>feathers</u>?

B: Yes, a <u>parrot</u> has <u>feathers</u>.

B: Does a <u>lion</u> have <u>scales</u>?

A: No, a <u>lion</u> doesn't have <u>scales</u>.

A: Does a _____ have _____?

B: Yes, a _____ has _____.

B: Does a _____ have _____?

A: No, a _____ doesn't have _____.

E Think Critically

Talk with your class.

List. Look at the charts.

1. How many animals have a tail? Name them.

2. How many animals have scales? Name them.

Compare. Look at the charts.

1. How are a fish and a snake the same?

2. Pick two other animals. How are they the same?

125

1. predict
predecir

2. test
probar

3. pour
verter

4. record
registrar

5. compare
comparar

6. graph
la gráfica

7. sort
clasificar

8. diagram
el diagrama

9. chart
la tabla

10. explain
explicar

Sequence Steps in a Process

 **Use** *first* **and** *then* **to talk about steps in science.**

First, predict.
Then, test.

First, pour water.
Then, record the amount.

First, make a chart.
Then, explain the chart.

Talk about steps in science.

_____, sort objects.

_____, draw a diagram.

_____, compare weights.

_____, make a graph.

First, _____.
Then, _____.

 1. solid
el sólido

 4. wood
la madera

 7. mix
mezclar

 2. liquid
el líquido

 5. metal
el metal

 8. sink
hundir

 3. gas
el gas

 6. ice
el hielo

 9. float
flotar

Discuss Matter

10. freeze
congelar

11. melt
derretir

12. boil
hervir

Use **verbs** to ask and answer questions about matter.

A: Does water <u>freeze</u>?

B: Yes, water <u>freezes</u>.

Ask and answer questions about matter.

A: Does ice melt?

B: Yes, ice _____.

B: Does _____?

A: _____.

129

54 Heat, Light, and Sound

El calor, la luz, y el sonido

1. guitar
la guitarra

4. piano
el piano

7. iron
la plancha

2. drum
el tambor

5. oven
el horno

8. candle
la vela

3. whistle
el silbato

6. grill
la parrilla

9. prism
el prisma

OXFORD CRAFT FAIR

Identify Sources

10. rainbow
el arco iris

11. reflection
el reflejo

12. shadow
la sombra

Use *source of* to talk about heat, light, and sound.

The whistle is a <u>source of</u> sound.
The iron is a <u>source of</u> heat.
The candle is a <u>source of</u> light.

Talk about heat, light, and sound.

The oven is a _____ heat.
The lamp is a _____ light.
The _____ is a source of sound.
The _____ is a source of _____.

131

55 Motion and Force
El movimiento y la fuerza

 1. slide
la resbaladilla

 4. magnet
el imán

 7. drop
soltar

 2. swing
el columpio

 5. attract
atraer

 **8.** push
empujar

 3. wheels
las ruedas

 6. roll
rodar

 **9.** pull
tirar

Describe Action

10. speed up
acelerar

11. slow down
desacelerar

12. stop
detener

Use a verb with *-ing* to talk about what someone or something is doing.

The ball is <u>rolling</u>.
The girl is <u>going</u> down the slide.
The boy is <u>speeding</u> up.

Talk about what people and things are doing.

The woman is _____ the swing.
The boy is _____ the wagon.
_____ is _____.

56 Energy and Electricity

La energía y la electricidad

1. lawn mower
la cortadora
de pasto

2. fan
el ventilador

3. flashlight
la linterna

4. light bulb
la bombilla
de luz

5. wire
el cable

6. cord
el cordón

7. plug
el enchufe

8. outlet
el tomacorriente

9. light switch
el interruptor
de la luz

Identify Energy Sources

10. gas
la gasolina

11. battery
la batería

12. electricity
la electricidad

Use *runs on* to talk about things that use energy.

The fan <u>runs on</u> electricity.
The flashlight <u>runs on</u> batteries.
The lawn mower <u>runs on</u> gas.

Talk about things that use energy.

The toy dog _____ batteries.
The lamp runs on _____.
The _____ runs on _____.

135

A Read a Chart

Look at the Sources of Energy chart.

Sources of Energy

	heat	light	sound
light bulb		X	
guitar			X
iron	X		
candle	X	X	
flashlight		X	

B Discuss

Talk about the chart. Take turns.

A <u>light bulb</u> is a source of light.

A <u>candle</u> is a source of heat and light.

A <u>guitar</u> is a source of _____.

A _____ is a source of _____.

C Make a Chart

Complete the chart in your notebook.

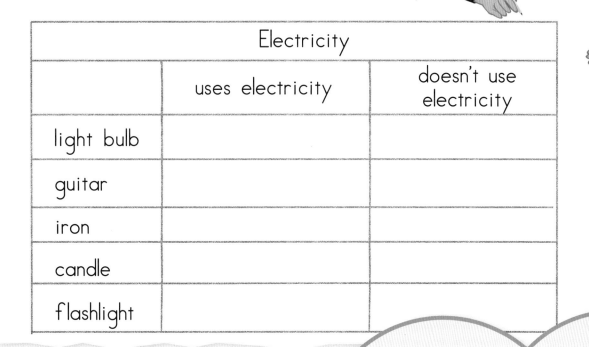

Electricity		
	uses electricity	doesn't use electricity
light bulb		
guitar		
iron		
candle		
flashlight		

D Discuss

Ask and answer questions about your chart. Take turns.

A: Does an <u>iron</u> use electricity?

B: Yes, it uses electricity.

B: Does a <u>candle</u> use electricity?

A: No, it doesn't use electricity.

A: Does a _____ use electricity?

B: Yes, _____.

B: Does a _____ use electricity?

A: No, _____.

E Think Critically

Talk with your class.

List. Look at the charts.

1. What is a source of light?

2. What uses electricity?

Make Connections. Look at the charts.

1. Which things use electricity and give light?

2. What other things do you know that use electricity?

1. mountain

la montaña

2. volcano

el volcán

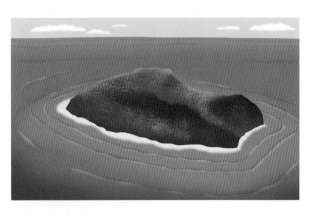

3. island

la isla

4. peninsula

la península

5. bay

la bahía

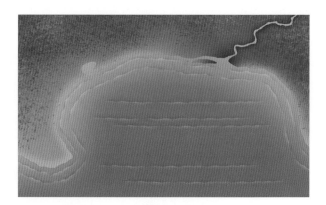

6. gulf

el golfo

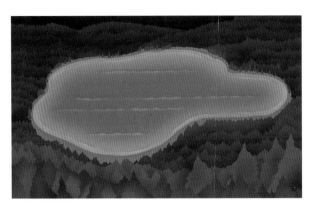

7. lake
el lago

8. plain
la llanura

9. plateau
la meseta

10. canyon
el cañón

Classify Earth Features

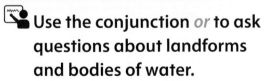 **Use the conjunction _or_ to ask questions about landforms and bodies of water.**

A: Is a bay a landform <u>or</u> a body of water?

B: It's a body of water.

B: Is an island a landform <u>or</u> a body of water?

A: It's a landform.

Ask and answer questions about landforms and bodies of water.

A: Is a plain a landform or a body of water?

B: It's a _____.

B: Is a _____ a landform or a body of water?

A: It's a _____.

139

1. mountain range
la cordillera

2. glacier
el glaciar

3. cliff
el acantilado

4. hill
la colina

5. valley
el valle

6. waterfall
la catarata

7. dam
el dique

8. cave
la cueva

9. steep
empinado/a

Describe the Landforms

10. level
llano/a

11. high
alto/a

12. low
bajo/a

Use adjectives to talk about the landforms.

The mountain range is <u>high</u>.
The valley is <u>low</u>.
The plain is <u>level</u>.

Talk about the landforms.

The _____ is steep.
The waterfall is _____.
The _____ is _____.

59 Earth Materials
Los materiales de la Tierra

VOLCANO ERUPTION
Erupción volcánica

 1. rocks
las rocas

 4. crystal
el cristal

 7. clay
la arcilla

 2. pebble
la piedrecita

 5. soil
la tierra

 8. lava
la lava

 3. boulder
la roca

 6. mud
el lodo

 9. models
los modelos

EROSION
Erosión

WEATHERING
Meteorización

Describe Earth Materials

10. layer
la capa

11. hard
duro/a

12. soft
blando/a

Use adjectives to talk about earth materials.

The crystal is <u>hard</u>.

The clay is <u>soft</u>.

The boulder is <u>large</u>.

The pebble is <u>small</u>.

Talk about earth materials.

The _____ is soft.

The _____ is hard.

The _____ is _____.

143

Dinosaurs and Fossils

Los dinosaurios y los fósiles

Tyrannosaurus rex

Stegosaurus

 1. dinosaurs
los dinosaurios

 4. horn
el cuerno

 7. fossil
el fósil

 2. skeleton
el esqueleto

 5. spike
la púa

 8. plant-eater
herbívoro/a

 3. skull
el cráneo

 6. footprint
la huella

 9. meat-eater
carnívoro/a

Diplodocus

Triceratops

Describe Dinosaurs

10. scientist
la científica

11. sharp
filoso/a

12. flat
plano/a

Use the verb _had_ to talk about dinosaurs.

Triceratops <u>had</u> horns.
Plant-eaters <u>had</u> flat teeth.
Tyrannosaurus rex <u>had</u> sharp teeth.

Talk about the dinosaurs.

Tyrannosaurus rex _____ a large skull.
Meat-eaters had _____ teeth.
Stegosaurus had _____.
_____ had _____.

145

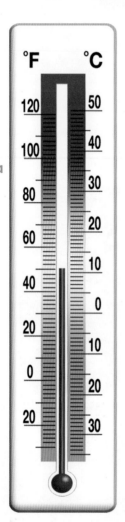

hot
caluroso/a

warm
cálido/a

cool
fresco/a

cold
frío/a

Seattle

San Francisco

Denv

Los Angeles

1. temperature
la temperatura

4. snow
la nieve

7. fog
la niebla

2. sunshine
el sol

5. hail
el granizo

8. lightning
el rayo

3. rain
la lluvia

6. wind
el viento

9. thunderstorm
la tormenta
eléctrica

Minneapolis

New York

St. Louis

Oklahoma City

Dallas

Miami

Describe Weather in the Past

Use the verb *was* to talk about yesterday's weather.

There <u>was</u> fog in San Francisco.
There <u>was</u> rain in Seattle.
There <u>was</u> a blizzard in Minneapolis.

Talk about the weather.

There was _____ in Dallas.
There was _____ in New York.
There was _____ in _____.

10. hurricane
el huracán

11. tornado
el tornado

12. blizzard
la ventisca

147

62 On the Coast

En la costa

1. wave
la ola

4. pond
la laguna

7. vapor
el vapor

2. river
el río

5. salt water
el agua salada

8. cloud
la nube

3. stream
el arroyo

6. fresh water
el agua dulce

9. drops
las gotas

Water Cycle
el ciclo del agua

10. evaporation
la evaporación

11. condensation
la condensación

12. precipitation
la precipitación

Use the adverb *also* **to talk about water.**

A river has fresh water.
A pond <u>also</u> has fresh water.

Evaporation is part of the water cycle.
Condensation is <u>also</u> part of the water cycle.

Talk about water.

Vapor is part of the water cycle.

_____ is <u>also</u> part of the water cycle.

149

1. pollution
la contaminación

4. litter
los desperdicios

7. glass
el vidrio

2. smog
el smog

5. garbage
la basura

8. plastic
el plástico

3. exhaust
los gases de
combustión

6. cardboard
el cartón

9. aluminum
el aluminio

Describe Action

10. bins
los basureros

11. recycle
reciclar

12. throw away
botar a la
basura

Use a verb with *-ing* to talk about what someone is doing.

She is <u>picking</u> up litter.
He is <u>recycling</u> cardboard.
She is <u>throwing</u> away trash.

Talk about what the people are doing.

He is _____ the plastic.
She is _____ the glass.
_____ is _____.

151

Sun
Sol

Mercury
Mercurio

Venus
Venus

Earth
Tierra

Mars
Marte

Jupiter
Júpiter

 1. solar system
el Sistema Solar

 4. orbit
la órbita

 7. star
la estrella

 2. planets
los planetas

 5. moon phases
las fases de
la luna

 8. constellation
la constelación

 3. moon
la luna

 6. ring
el anillo

 9. comet
el cometa

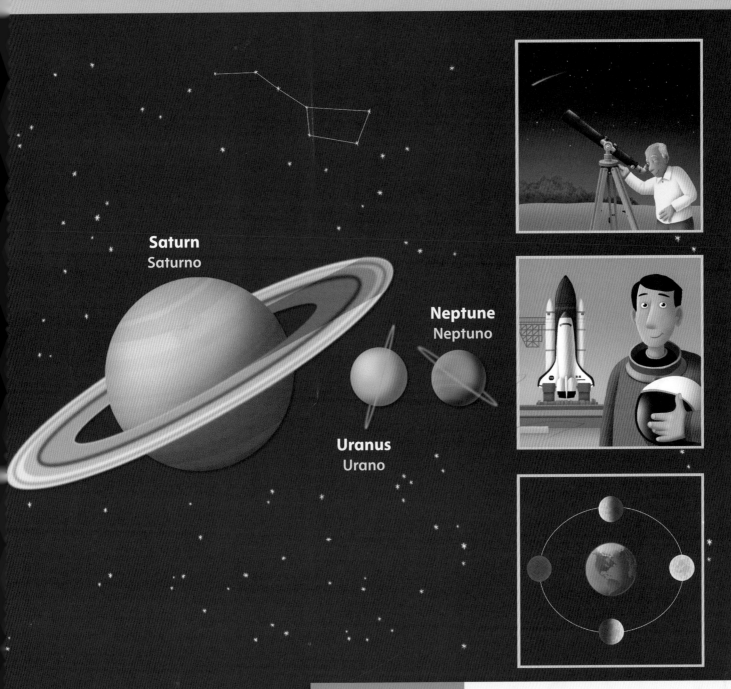

Saturn
Saturno

Neptune
Neptuno

Uranus
Urano

Discuss Space

10. telescope
el telescopio

11. rocket
el cohete

12. astronaut
el astronauta

 Use *What is* _____*? **to ask questions about space.**

A: <u>What is</u> Mercury?

B: Mercury is a planet.

B: <u>What is</u> a constellation?

A: A constellation is a group of stars.

Ask and answer questions about space.

A: What is _____?

B: _____.

A Read a Diagram

Look at the Earth Features diagram.

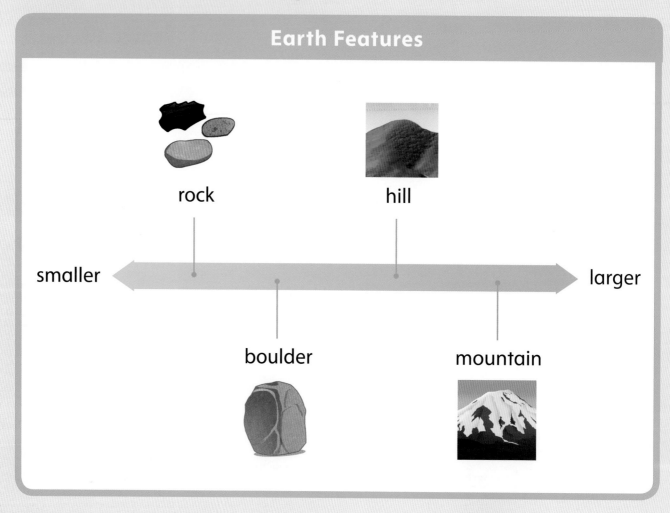

Earth Features

rock

hill

smaller ← → larger

boulder

mountain

B Discuss

Talk about the diagram. Take turns.

A <u>boulder</u> is smaller than a <u>hill</u>.

A <u>mountain</u> is larger than a <u>rock</u>.

A <u>hill</u> is smaller than a _____.

A _____ is larger than a _____.

A _____ is _____ than a _____.

C Make a Diagram

Complete the diagram in your notebook.

Bodies of Water

Word Box
drop
gulf
lake
pond

smaller ← → larger

D Discuss

👥 **Ask and answer questions about your diagram. Take turns.**

A: Is a <u>lake</u> smaller than a <u>gulf</u>?

B: Yes, a <u>lake</u> is smaller than a <u>gulf</u>.

B: Is a <u>pond</u> larger than a <u>lake</u>?

A: No, a <u>pond</u> isn't larger than a <u>lake</u>.

A: Is a _____ smaller than a _____?

B: _____.

B: Is a _____ larger than a _____?

A: _____.

E Think Critically

👥 **Talk with your class.**

Identify. Look at the diagrams.

1. What is the smallest earth feature?

2. What is the largest body of water?

Make Connections. Look at the diagrams.

1. What is smaller than a rock?

2. What is larger than a gulf?

1. five o'clock
las cinco en punto

2. five fifteen
las cinco y cuarto

3. five thirty
las cinco y media

4. five forty-five
las seis menos cuarto

5. hour hand
el horario

6. minute hand
el minutero

7. hour
la hora

8. minute
el minuto

9. a.m.
a. m.

10. p.m.
p. m.

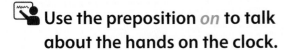 **Use the preposition *on* to talk about the hands on the clock.**

A: The hour hand is <u>on</u> the 5.
The minute hand is <u>on</u> the 12.
What time is it?

B: It's 5:00.

B: The hour hand is <u>on</u> the 5.
The minute hand is <u>on</u> the 9.
What time is it?

A: It's 5:45.

Talk about the clock.

A: The hour hand is _____ the 5.
The minute hand is _____ the 3.
What time is it?

B: It's 5:15.

B: The hour hand is on the _____.
The minute hand is on the _____.
What time is it?

A: It's _____.

2+3=5 **1. problem**
el problema

✖ **4. multiply**
multiplicar

② ④ **7. even numbers**
⑥ ⑧ los números pares

➕ **2. add**
sumar

➗ **5. divide**
dividir

① ③ **8. odd numbers**
⑤ ⑦ los números
impares

➖ **3. subtract**
restar

➖ **6. equals**
es igual a

0 1 2 3 4 **9. number line**
la recta numérica

Read Math Problems

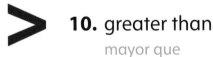

10. greater than
mayor que

11. less than
menor que

12. count
contar

Use these words to read math symbols.

+	2 + 3	two <u>plus</u> three
−	5 – 2	five <u>minus</u> two
×	2 × 3	two <u>times</u> three
÷	6 ÷ 2	six <u>divided by</u> two
=	2 + 3 = 5	two plus three <u>equals</u> five

Use symbols to make math problems.
Then read.

5 _____ 3 = _____

6 _____ 3 = _____

159

67 Shapes

Las figuras y los cuerpos geométricos

CRACKERS

1. circle
el círculo

4. rectangle
el rectángulo

7. pyramid
la pirámide

2. triangle
el triángulo

5. pentagon
el pentágono

8. cube
el cubo

3. square
el cuadrado

6. sphere
la esfera

9. cylinder
el cilindro

160 Unit 9 Math

Describe Shapes

10. cone
el cono

11. side
el lado

12. angle
el ángulo

Use numbers to talk about shapes.

A triangle has <u>three</u> sides.
A square has <u>four</u> angles.
A pentagon has <u>five</u> sides.

Talk about shapes.

A rectangle has _____ angles.
A _____ has _____ sides.
A _____ has _____ angles.
A _____ has _____.

161

68 Fractions and Decimals

Las fracciones y los decimales

PLACE VALUE

3.1

3.14

3.141

 1. whole
un entero

 2. one half
un medio

 3. one third
un tercio

 4. one fourth
un cuarto

1,2,3 **5.** whole numbers
los números
enteros

$\frac{1}{2}$ $\frac{1}{3}$ $\frac{1}{4}$ **6.** fractions
las fracciones

$\rightarrow \dfrac{1}{4}$ **7.** numerator
el numerador

$\dfrac{1}{4}\leftarrow$ **8.** denominator
el denominador

 9. equal parts
las partes
iguales

WHOLE
1.0

1

HALF
0.5

$\frac{1}{2}$	$\frac{1}{2}$

THIRD
0.33

$\frac{1}{3}$	$\frac{1}{3}$	$\frac{1}{3}$

FOURTH
0.25

$\frac{1}{4}$	$\frac{1}{4}$	$\frac{1}{4}$	$\frac{1}{4}$

$$\frac{\frac{1}{4}}{\frac{1}{4}} = \frac{1}{2}$$

$$\frac{2}{4} = \frac{1}{2}$$

Discuss Fractions

0.25 **10.** decimal point
↑   el punto decimal

0.25 **11.** tenths place
↑   el lugar de
            los décimos

0.25 **12.** hundredths place
↑   el lugar de
            los centésimos

Use *does* and *doesn't* to ask and answer questions about fractions.

A: <u>Does</u> he have one whole circle?

B: Yes, he <u>does</u>.

B: <u>Does</u> she have one fourth of a circle?

A: No, she <u>doesn't</u>. She has one third of a circle.

Ask and answer questions about fractions.

A: Does _____ have _____?

B: _____.

69 Measurement
La medición

 1. inch
la pulgada

 4. centimeter
el centímetro

 7. pint
la pinta

 2. foot
el pie

 5. meter
el metro

 8. quart
el cuarto

 3. yard
la yarda

 6. cup
la taza

 9. gallon
el galón

164 Unit 9 Math

10. liter
el litro

11. ounce
la onza

12. gram
el gramo

Compare Units of Measure

Use adjectives with _–er_ to talk about units of measure.

A meter is <u>longer</u> than a centimeter.
A gallon is <u>larger</u> than a cup.
Five ounces is <u>heavier</u> than one ounce.

Talk about units of measure.

A pint is _____ than a quart.
An inch is _____ than a _____.
_____ is _____ than a _____.

165

1, 2, 3...

MONEY	VALUE
	1¢
	5¢
	10¢
	25¢
	100¢

 1. penny
la moneda
de 1¢

 2. nickel
la moneda
de 5¢

 3. dime
la moneda
de 10¢

 4. quarter
la moneda
de 25¢

 5. dollar
el dólar

1¢ 6. cent
el centavo

 7. coins
las monedas

 8. bills
los billetes

 9. price
el precio

Discuss Value

10. buy
comprar

11. sell
vender

12. save
ahorrar

Use *How much _____?* to ask about money.

A: <u>How much</u> is a nickel worth?
B: A nickel is worth 5 cents.

B: <u>How much</u> is a quarter worth?
A: A quarter is worth 25 cents.

Ask and answer questions about money.

A: How much is a _____ worth?
B: A _____ is worth _____.

167

A Read a Diagram

Look at the Fractions diagram.

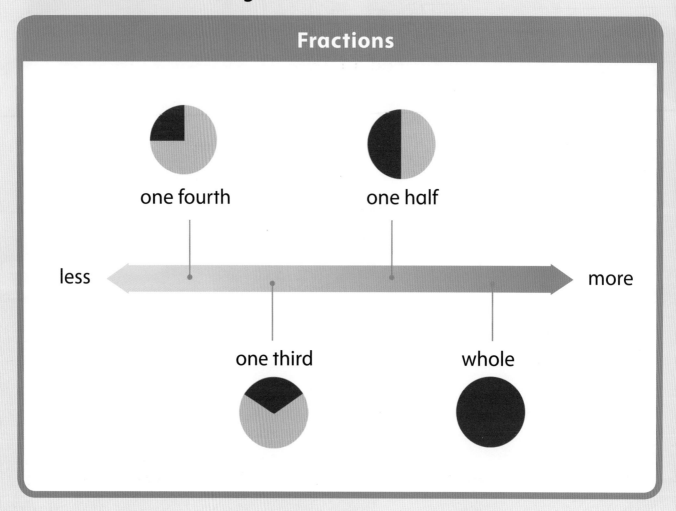

Fractions

one fourth

one half

less ⟵ ⟶ more

one third

whole

B Discuss

👥 **Talk about the diagram. Take turns.**

One half is more than one third.

One fourth is less than one half.

One whole is more than _____.

_____ is less than _____.

_____ is _____ than _____.

C Make a Diagram

Complete the diagram in your notebook.

Liquid Measures

Word Box

cup

gallon

pint

quart

less ←————————————————→ more

D Discuss

👥 **Ask and answer questions about your diagram. Take turns.**

A: Is a <u>quart</u> more than a <u>cup</u>?

B: Yes, it is more than a <u>cup</u>.

B: Is a <u>gallon</u> less than a <u>pint</u>?

A: No, it isn't less than a <u>pint</u>.

A: Is a _____ more than a _____?

B: _____.

B: Is a _____ less than a _____?

A: _____.

E Think Critically

👥 **Talk with your class.**

Apply. Look at both diagrams.

1. What is the smallest fraction?

2. What is the largest liquid measure?

Make Connections. Look at both diagrams.

1. When do you use fractions and liquid measures together?

2. How else do you use fractions?

169

Index

The number(s) to the right of each entry tell the page(s) the words are on. Page numbers in pink show labels from the pictures.

A

above 10
acorn 118
across from 11
add 158
address 58
afternoon 6
airplane 70
airport 70
alarm clock 20
aluminum 150
a.m. 157
ambulance 74
angle 161
angry 52
ankle 96, 99
answer questions 35
ant 120
antelope 111
antlers 111
apartment
   building 58
apple 64
April 5
arm 97
around 11
art room 37
ask questions 35
astronaut 153
atlas 42
attract 132
August 5
aunt 17
avocado 64

B

baby 75
back 96
backpack 39
bag 46
ballot 87

balls 48
bananas 24
bandage 50
bangs 14
bank 62
bark 118
barn 78
baseball cap 29
basket 48
bat 120
bathing suit 31
bathroom 19
bathtub 22
battery 76, 135
bay 138
be born 82
beak 110
bear 118
beans 103, 109
bed 20
bedroom 19
bee 109
behind 10
below 10
bench 59
between 10
bicycle 68
bills 166
binder 39
binoculars 106
bins 151
bird 113
bison 110
black 7
blanket 20
bleed 50
blizzard 147
blowhole 115
blue 7
board 40
boats 72

boil 129
bone 98
book 39
bookshelves 42
boots 30
border 84
bottle 46
boulder 142
bounce 48
bowl 67
box 65
brain 98
bread 25
bridge 72
broccoli 66
brother 16
brown 7
brush 23
brush teeth 13
bud 108
build houses 56
building 68
bulb 109
bus 68
bus driver 36
bus stop 68
butter 25
butterfly 112
buy 167

C

cabinet 24
cactus 116
cafeteria 37
cafeteria worker 37
calculator 38
call 911 77
call number 42
can 46
candle 130
canyon 139

capital 84
Capitol 88
car 68
cardboard 150
carrots 46
cart 65
carton 46
cashier 62
cast 74
cat 112
catalog 42
catch 48
caterpillar 112
cave 140
celebrate 83
celery 64
cent 166
centimeter 164
cereal 25
chair 40
chart 127
check out 43
cheek 95
cheese 103
chest 96
chick 113
chicken 66, 78
chin 95
circle 160
citizen 86
city 86
city council 86
classroom 37
claw 110
clay 142
clean 9
click 45
cliff 140
climb 49
clock 40
closed 8
closet 20
cloud 148
coach 37
cocoon 112

coins 166
cold 9, 146
colored pencil 38
comb 22
comb hair 12
comet 152
compare 126
compass rose 85
computer 44
computer lab 37
condensation 149
cone 161
confused 52
Congress 88
constellation 152
continent 84
cook 19
cool 146
coral 114
cord 134
corn 102
corner 58
cough 51
council member 86
count 159
counter 24
country 84, 86
court 48, 87
courtroom 86
cousin 17
cover mouth 93
cow 78
coyote 116
crab 114
crackers 47
crane 72
crayon 38
crops 78
cross the street 61
crossing guard 36
crosswalk 60
crutches 74
cry 53
crystal 142
cube 160

cup 24, 164
curly 15
cursor 44
custodian 37
customer 62
cut 50
cylinder 160

D

daisy 108
dam 140
dark 15
December 5
decimal point 163
deer 118
deliver mail 56
denominator 162
desk 20
diagram 127
dictionary 42
die 82
different 9
dime 166
dinosaurs 144
Diplodocus 145
dirty 9
divide 158
do homework 13
dock 72
doctor 75
dollar 166
dolphin 114
door 18
down 11
dragonfly 120
draw 34
drawer 20
dress 28
dresser 20
drink water 92
drive 69
drop 132
drops 148
drugstore 62
drum 130
dry 9, 23

dunes 117
DVD 42

E

eagle 88
earache 50
ear 95
Earth 152
eat 19
eat breakfast 12
eat dinner 13
egg 112
eggs 24
eight 2
eighteen 2
eighth 4
eighty 3
elbow 99
election 87
electricity 135
elephant 122
eleven 2
emergency
  room 74
empty 9
equal parts 162
equals 158
equator 84
eraser 38
erosion 143
eruption 142
escape route 77
evaporation 149
even numbers 158
evening 6
exercise 92
exhaust 150
exit 77
explain 127
explore 82
eyebrow 94
eyelashes 14
eyelid 94
eyes 14

F

factory 71
fall 31, 49
fan 134
farmer 78
fast 8
father 16
feather 110
February 5
feed 79
feel 100
fence 59
fern 121
ferry 72
fever 50
field 48, 78
fifteen 2
fifth 4
fifty 3
fight fires 57
fin 114
finger 98
fingernail 99
fire escape 76
fire extinguisher 76
fire truck 76
firefighter 76
first 4
fish 103
five 2
five fifteen 156
five forty-five 156
five o'clock 156
five thirty 156
fix cars 56
flag 41
flamingo 122
flashlight 134
flat 145
float 128
floor 19
floss 92
flowers 108
fog 146
foot 96, 164
footprint 144

forehead 94
fork 66
forty 3
fossil 144
four 2
fourteen 2
fourth 4
fractions 162
freeze 129
fresh water 148
Friday 5
frog 112
frown 52
fruits 103
full 9
fur 110

G

gallon 164
garbage 150
garden 68
gas 128, 135
gas station 63
get a checkup 93
get dressed 12
gills 114
giraffe 123
glacier 140
glass 150
glasses 14
globe 41
gloves 30
glue 40
go to bed 13
go to the dentist 92
gorilla 111
governor 86
grains 103
grandfather 16
grandmother 16
grandparents 16
gram 165
grapes 24
graph 126
grass 12
gray 7

great-
　grandmother 16
greater than 159
green 7
grill 130
groceries 63
grow crops 57
guitar 130
gulf 138
gums 94
gym 37

H

hail 146
hair 14
hand 97
happy 52
hard 143
hat 30
hatch 113
hawk 116
head 96
headphones 44
hear 100
hearing 101
heart 98
heavy 9
helicopter 70
helmet 68
help 27
hemisphere 84
high 141
highway 70
hill 140
hip 99
hippopotamus 122
hole 117
hoof 111
horn 144
horse 78
hot 9, 146
hour 157
hour hand 156
house 58
hundredths
　place 163

hurricane 147
hyena 122

I

ice 128
immigrate 83
in 10
in front of 10
inch 164
Internet 44
intersection 60
invent 83
iris 109
iron 130
island 138

J

jacket 31
jaguar 120
January 5
jeans 28
judge 86
juice 47
July 5
jump 48
June 5
Jupiter 152

K

kangaroo 110
key 84
keyboard 44
kick 48
kitchen 19
kitten 112
knee 96
knife 66

L

lake 139
lamp 18
large 8
laugh 53
laundry 63
lava 142
lawn mower 134

layer 143
leaders 86
leaf 108
left 8
leg 96
lemon 64
leopard 122
less than 159
lettuce 64
level 141
librarian 36
library 37
library card 42
lie down 51
life jacket 73
light 9, 15
light bulb 134
light switch 134
lighthouse 72
lightning 146
Lincoln
　Memorial 89
lion 122
lips 94
liquid 128
list 64
listen 26
liter 165
litter 150
living room 18
lizard 116
load 73
log in 45
long 14
look 43
loud 101
low 141
lungs 98

M

magazine 42
magnet 132
magnifying
　glass 106
mailbox 61
mail carrier 60

map 41
March 5
marker 38
Mars 152
matches 76
May 5
mayor 86
measure 106
measuring cup 107
measuring tape 107
meat 103
meat-eater 144
meeting 87
melt 129
menu 66
Mercury 152
metal 128
meter 164
meter stick 107
microphone 44
microscope 106
midnight 6
milk 47, 103
minute 157
minute hand 156
mirror 18
mix 128
models 142
Monday 5
monitor 44
monkey 111
monument 88
moon 152
moon phases 152
morning 6
mosquito 119
moss 121
moth 120
mother 16
motorcycle 70
mountain 138
mountain
  range 140
mouse 44, 116
mouth 94

movie theater 60
mud 142
multiply 158
muscle 98
museum 60
music 26
music room 37

N
napkin 67
national anthem 89
neck 96
needles 118
Neptune 153
nest 112
new 8
newspaper 42
next to 10
nickel 166
night 6
nine 2
nineteen 2
ninety 3
ninth 4
noon 6
nose 94
notebook 40
November 5
number line 158
numerator 162
nurse 36
nursery 75
nurse's office 37
nuts 103

O
oak tree 118
oatmeal 102
observe 106
ocean 84
October 5
octopus 114
office 37
old 8
on 10
one 2

one fourth 162
one half 162
one hundred 3
one third 162
open 8
operating room 75
orange 7, 64
orbit 152
orchard 78
orchid 121
order 67
ounce 165
outlet 134
oven 130
over 11
owl 120

P
pajamas 28
pants 28
paper 40, 150
paper towels 65
paramedic 74
parents 16
park 59
parrot 120
pasta 102
patient 74
paw 110
peach 102
pear 102
pebble 142
pen 38
pencil 38
pencil sharpener 38
peninsula 138
penny 166
pentagon 160
peppers 102
petal 108
pharmacist 62
phone 26
piano 130
pick 79
pick up 21
picture 18

pillow 20
pineapple 64
pine cone 118
pine tree 118
pink 7
pint 164
plain 139
planets 152
plant-eater 144
plastic 150
plate 24
plateau 139
play 27
Pledge of
  Allegiance 88
plow 79
plug 134
p.m. 157
police car 70
police officer 60
police station 60
pollen 109
pollution 150
pond 148
ponytail 14
post office 60
pouch 110
pour 126
prairie dog 116
precipitation 149
predict 126
president 86
price 166
principal 36
printer 44
prism 130
problem 158
protect the
  community 57
pull 132
purple 7
push 132
put away 21
puzzle 21
pyramid 160

Q
quart 164
quarter 166
quiet 101

R
rabbit 116
radio 26
rain 146
rainbow 131
raincoat 30
raise animals 57
raise hand 34
ray 114
read 34
receptionist 74
record 126
rectangle 160
recycle 151
red 7
reflection 131
refrigerator 24
remote 26
repeat 34
restroom 37
return 43
ribs 98
rice 66
ride 69
right 8
ring 152
river 148
rocket 153
rocks 142
roll 132
roots 108
rose 108
rough 100
rug 26
ruler 40, 106
run 49

S
sad 52
sailboat 72
salad 46

salesperson 62
salt water 148
same 9
sand 117
sandals 31
sandwich 46
Saturday 5
Saturn 153
save 167
scale 85
scales 115
scared 52
scarf 30
scientist 145
scissors 38
scorpion 116
seat belt 68
seaweed 114
second 4
secretary 36
see 100
seedling 108
seeds 108
sell 167
sell clothing 56
September 5
serve food 56
server 66
seven 2
seventeen 2
seventh 4
seventy 3
shadow 131
shampoo 22
shark 114
sharp 145
shell 111
shiny 100
ship 72
shoe store 62
shoes 29
short 8, 14
shorts 30
shot 74
shoulder 96, 99

side 161
sidewalk. 58
sight. 100
sign 71
sign a document. 82
silly. 95
sink 18, 128
sister 16
six 2
sixteen 2
sixth. 4
sixty 3
skeleton 99, 144
skin 98
skip counting 159
skirt 28
skull 99, 144
skyscraper. 71
sleep 92
slide 132
slow 8
slow down. 133
small 8
smell 100
smile 52
smiling 94
smog 150
smoke 76
smoke detector 76
smooth 100
snake 116
sneakers. 29
sneeze. 51
snow 146
soap 22
socks 28
sofa 26
soft. 143
soil 142
solar system 152
solid. 128
sore throat 50
sort. 127
soup 66
sour 101

speech 87
speed up 133
sphere 160
spider 120
spike 144
spinach. 102
spoon 66
spots 123
spring 30
square. 160
squirrel 119
stairs 18
star. 152
Star Spangled
    Banner. 89
stars. 89
state 84, 86
Statue of Liberty 88
steep 140
Stegosaurus 144
stem. 108
stomach. 98
stomachache. 50
stop 133
stop sign 58
stove 24
straight. 14
strawberries 46
stream 148
street 58
streetlight 58
street sign 58
stripes 89, 123
student. 36
study 27
subtract 158
summer 31
Sun. 152
Sunday 5
sunflower. 109
sunglasses. 30
sunshine 146
supermarket. 62
Supreme Court 88
surgeon 75

surprised 52
sweater. 30
sweatshirt 28
sweet. 100
sweet potato 102
swing. 132
symbols 85

T

table 18
tadpole. 112
tail 110
take a bath 12
take a shower 12
take care of
    people 56
talk. 26
tall 8
tan 7
tape. 40
taste 100
taxi. 61
teacher. 36
teacher's aide. 36
teeth 94
telescope. 153
television 26
teller 62
temperature. 146
ten 2
tentacles 115
tenth 4
tenths place 163
test. 126
thermometer. . . 50, 107
think 34
third. 4
thirteen. 2
thirty 3
thorn 108
three 2
through 11
throw. 48
throw away. 151
Thursday 5
thunderstorm. 146

tiger 110
tired 52
tissues 50
toe 99
toenail 99
toilet 22
tomato 64, 109
tongue 94
toothbrush 22
toothpaste 22
tornado 147
touch 100
towel 22
toys 20
tractor 78
trade 82
traffic light 60
train 70
trash can 40
travel 82
tray 46
triangle 160
Triceratops 145
truck 70
trunk 118
T-shirt 28
Tuesday 5
tugboat 72
tulip 109
turtle 120
twelve 2
twenty 2
twenty-five 3
twenty-four 3
twenty-one 3
twenty-three 3
twenty-two 3
two 2
type 45
Tyrannosaurus
    rex 144

U
umbrella 30
uncle 17
under 11

underwear 28
uniform 76
unload 73
up 11
Uranus 153
use a tissue 93

V
valley 140
value 166
van 70
vapor 148
vegetables 103
Venus 152
volcano 138, 142
vote 87

W
wait 68
waiting room 74
wake up 12
walk 69
wall 18
warm 146
wash 23
wash hands 92
Washington
    Monument 88
water 22
water cycle 149
waterfall 140
watering hole 122
wave 148
wear sunblock 93
weathering 143
Wednesday 5
wet 9
wheelchair 74
wheels 132
whiskers 110
whistle 130
white 7
White House 88
whole 162
whole numbers 162
wind 146

window 18
wing 110
winter 30
wire 134
wood 128
woodpecker 119
work in a group 35
work with a
    partner 35
wrist 97, 99
write 34

X
X-ray 74

Y
yard 164
yawn 53
yellow 7
yogurt 102

Z
zebra 122

Índice

Los números ubicados a la derecha de cada entrada indican la página en la cual se presenta el término. Los números de página de color rosado indican rótulos o texto utilizados en las ilustraciones principales de cada tema.

A

a través de........ 11
a. m.............. 157
abajo............. 11
abeja............ 109
abierto/a 8
abrevadero....... 122
abril................5
abuela 16
abuelo 16
abuelos 16
acantilado........ 140
acelerar 133
acera............ 58
adulto/a.......... 113
aeropuerto 70
agosto..............5
agotar........... 150
agua dulce 148
agua salada...... 148
agua 22
aguacate.......... 64
águila 88
agujas........... 118
ahorrar.......... 167
al lado de......... 10
ala 110
alcalde 86
aleta 114
alga marina 114
alimentar......... 79
almohada 20
alrededor......... 11
alto/a 8, 141
aluminio......150, 150

amargo/a 101
amarillo 7
ambulancia 74
anaranjado........ 64
ángulo 161
anillo............ 152
antílope 111
apio 64
araña 120
arar 79
arcilla 142
arco iris.......... 131
ardilla 119
arena............ 117
armario 20, 24
arriba 11
arroyo 148
arroz 66
áspero/a 100
astronauta 153
asustado/a 52
atlas............ 42
atraer 132
atrapar........... 48
auriculares 44
autobús 68
avena 102
avión............ 70
ayudante.......... 36
ayudar 27
ayuntamiento 86
azul 7

B

bahía............ 138
bajo............. 11

bajo/a.......8, 14, 141
bañarse 12
banco 59
banco 62
bandeja 46
bandera........... 41
baños 37
barbilla........... 95
barco............ 72
basura 150
basureros......... 151
batería 76, 135
bebé 75
beber agua........ 92
bellota 118
biblioteca 37
bibliotecaria....... 36
bicicleta 68
bigotes 110
billetes 166
binoculares........ 106
bisabuela.......... 16
bisonte 110
blanco..............7
blando/a 143
boca 94
bolsa 46, 110
bombero 76
bombilla de luz ... 134
bostezar.......... 53
botar a la basura . 151
botas............. 30
bote de la basura .. 40
botella 46
botes 72
branquias 114

brazo.............. 97
brillante 100
brócoli............ 66
bufanda........... 30
búho 120
bulbo............. 109
buzón 61

C

caballo 78
cabello 14
cabeza 96
cable 134
cactus 116
caer 132
caerse 31, 49
café 7
caja 65
cajera 62
cajero del banco... 62
calcetines......... 28
calculadora 38
cálido/a 147
calle.............. 58
caluroso/a......9, 147
cama............. 20
caminar 69
camión........... 70
camión de
    bomberos 76
camioneta........ 70
camiseta 28
camote.......... 102
campo 48, 78
canasta 48
cangrejo......... 114
canguro 110
cañón 139
cansado/a........ 52
cantina........... 37

capa 143
caparazón........ 111
capital............ 84
Capitolio 88
capullo 108, 112
cargar 73
carne............ 103
carnívoro/a 144
carpeta........... 39
carretera 70
carrito 65
carro 68
cartel............. 71
cartel indicador de
    la calle 58
cartera 60
cartón 150
Casa Blanca 88
casa............. 58
casco............. 68
catálogo.......... 42
catarata 140
catorce 2
cebra............ 122
ceja 94
celebrar 83
cenar............ 13
centavo 166
centímetro........ 164
cepillarse 23
cepillo de dientes .. 22
cerco 59
cereal 25
cereales 103
cerebro........... 98
cerillos............ 76
cerrado/a...........8
chaleco
    salvavidas....... 73
champú 22

chaqueta.......... 31
ciclo del agua..... 149
cien 3
científico 145
ciervo 118
cilindro 160
cinco 2
cinco en punto.... 156
cinco y cuarto 156
cinco y media..... 156
cincuenta...........3
cine 60
cinta adhesiva..... 40
cinta métrica 107
cinturón de
    seguridad 68
círculo........... 160
cirujano 75
ciudad........... 86
ciudadano........ 86
claro/a 15
clasificar......... 127
clave 84
cliente............ 62
cocina.........19, 24
cocinar 19
código de
    referencia 42
cohete........... 153
cola 110
coleta 14
colina 140
columpio 132
combatir
    incendios........ 57
comer 19
comerciar 82
cometa.......... 152
comparar........ 126
comprar......... 167

computadora 44
condensación 149
conducir 69
conductor de
    autobús 36
conejo 116
confundido/a 52
congelar 129
Congreso 88
cono 161
constelación 152
construir casas 56
contaminación . . . 150
contar 159
contar salteado . . . 159
continente 84
control remoto 26
coral 114
corazón 98
cordillera 140
cordón 134
correr 49
cortadora de
    pasto 134
Corte Suprema 88
corte 50
corteza 118
costillas 98
coyote 116
cráneo 144
crayola 38
criar animales 57
crisálida 113
cristal 142
cruce peatonal 60
cruzar la calle 61
cuaderno 40
cuadrado 160
cuarenta 3
cuatro 2

cuarto 164
cuarto/a 4
cuarto de baño 19
cubo 160
cubrirse la boca
    al toser 93
cuchara 66
cuchillo 66
cuello 96
cuernos 111, 144
cueva 140
cuidar a las
    personas 56
cultivar 57
cultivos 78
cursor 44

D
debajo 10
décimo/a 4
dedo 98
dedo del pie 99
delante de 10
delfín 114
denominador 162
dentrífico 22
derecha 8
derretir 129
desayunar 12
descargar 73
desperdicios 150
despertarse 12
detector de humo . . 76
detener 133
detrás 10
devolver un libro . . . 43
diagrama 127
dibujar 34
diccionario 42
diciembre 5
diecinueve 2

dieciocho 2
dieciséis 2
diecisiete 2
dientes 94
diez 2
diferente 9
dinosaurios 144
Diplodocus 145
dique 140
director 36
discurso 87
dividir 158
doce 2
doctora 75
dólar 166
dolor de estómago . 50
dolor de garganta . 50
dolor de oído 50
domicilio 58
domingo 5
dormir 92
dos 2
ducharse 12
dulce 100
dunas 117
durazno 102
duro/a 143
DVD 42

E
ecuador 84
edificio 68
edificio de
    apartamentos . . . 58
elección 87
electricidad 135
elefante 122
empinado/a 140

empleada de la
    cantina.......... 37
empujar.......... 132
en 10
enchufe 134
encías 94
encimera 24
enero..............5
enfermera 36
enfermería 37
enfrente de 11
enojado/a........ 52
ensalada 46
entero 162
entre 10
entregar el correo.. 56
entrenador 37
envase 46
erosión 142
erosionar 142
es igual a 158
escala 85
escalera de
    emergencia...... 76
escalera 18
escamas......... 115
escorpión........ 116
escribir 34, 45
escritorio 20
escuchar 26
esfera 160
espalda 96
espejo............ 18
esperar........... 68
espina........... 108
espinaca 102
esqueleto......99, 144
esquina 58
estación de
    policía.......... 60

estado.........84, 86
estanterías 42
Estatua de la
    Libertad 88
Estegosaurio...... 144
estómago 98
estornudar 51
estrella 152
estrellas 89
estudiante........ 36
estudiar 27
evaporación...... 149
explicar.......... 127
explorar 82
extinguidor de
    incendios....... 76

F

fábrica 71
falda 28
farmacéutica 62
farmacia 62
faro 72
farol............. 58
fases lunares 152
febrero 5
feliz 52
ferry............. 72
fiebre............. 50
filoso/a 145
firmar un
    documento...... 82
flamenco 122
flequillo 14
flores 108
flotar 128
fósil 144
fotografía 18
fracciones 162
frenar 133
frente............. 94

fresas............. 46
fresco/a 147
frijoles........103, 109
frío/a 9, 147
frontera 84
fruncir el ceño 52
frutas............ 103
frutos secos....... 103

G

galletas 47
galón............. 164
garra 110
gas..........128, 135
gasolinera........ 63
gatito............ 112
gato............. 112
gaveta 20
gimnasio 37
girasol........... 109
glaciar........... 140
globo terráqueo ... 41
gobernadora 86
golfo 138
goma de borrar.... 38
gorila............ 111
gorra 29
gotas 148
graficar.......... 126
gramo........... 165
grande 8
granero........... 78
granizo.......... 146
granjero.......... 78
gris................7
grúa............. 72
guantes 30
guardar 21
guardería......... 75
guitarra 130
gustar 100, 101

H

habano..............7
hablar............ 26
hacer clic 45
hacer ejercicio 92
hacer erupción ... 143
hacer la tarea...... 13
hacer preguntas ... 35
hacerse un
   chequeo........ 93
halcón............ 116
helecho........... 121
helicóptero 70
hemisferio 84
hermana 16
hermano 16
hervíboro/a...... 144
hervir............ 129
hielo............. 128
hiena............ 122
himno de los
   Estados Unidos .. 89
himno nacional.... 89
hipopótamo 122
hoja 108
hombro 96
hora............. 157
horario 156
hormiga 120
horno 130
huella 144
huerta........... 78
hueso 98
huevo 112
huevos 24, 113
húmedo/a..........9
humo............ 76
hundir........18, 128
huracán 147

I

igual 9
imán 132
impermeable 30
impresora 44
iniciar sesión....... 45
inmigrar.......... 83
inodoro.......... 22
Internet 44
interruptor de
   la luz 134
intersección 60
inventar 83
invierno 30
inyección 74
ir a dormir 13
ir al dentista 92
iris............... 109
isla 138
izquierda 8

J

jabón............. 22
jaguar........... 120
jardín............. 68
jeans 28
jirafa 123
jueves 5
jueza 86
jugar 27
jugo 47
juguetes.......... 20
julio 5
junio 5
Júpiter........... 153
Juramento a la
   Lealtad.......88, 88

L

labios 94

laboratorio de
   computación 37
lacio/a............ 14
lado 161
lagarto 116
lago 139
laguna 148
lámpara.......... 18
lanzar 48
lápiz............. 38
lápiz de color 38
largo/a 14
larva 113
lata............. 46
lava 142
lavandería......... 63
lavarse 23
lavarse las manos . 92
lavarse los dientes . 13
leche 47, 103
lechuga 64
leer.............. 34
lengua 94
lentes............. 14
lentes de sol 30
lento/a 8
león 122
leopardo 122
levantar la mano .. 34
libélula 120
libro 39
líderes 86
limón............. 64
limpiarse los dientes
   con hilo dental... 92
limpio/a 9
linterna.......... 134
líquido........... 128
lista 64
litro.............. 165

liviano/a 9
llamar al 911 77
llanura 139
lleno/a 9
llorar 53
lluvia 146
lodo 142
loro 120
lugar de los
    centésimos 163
lugar de los
    décimos 163
luna 152
lunes 5
lupa 106

M

madera 128
madre 16
madriguera 117
maestra 36
maíz 102
mañana 6
manchas 123
mano 97
manta 20
mantequilla 25
manzana 64
mapa 41
margarita 108
mariposa 112
Marte 153
martes 5
marzo 5
mayo 5
mayor que 159
medianoche 6
mediodía 6
medir 106

mejilla 95
menor que 159
menú 66
Mercurio 153
mesa 18
mesero 66
meseta 139
metal 128
metro 164
mezcla 128
micrófono 44
microscopio 106
miembro del
    ayuntamiento . . . 86
miércoles 5
minutero 156
minuto 157
mirar 43
mochila 39
modelos 142
moneda de 1¢ 166
moneda de 10¢ . . . 166
moneda de 25¢ . . . 166
moneda de 5¢ 166
monedas 166
monitor 44
mono 111
montaña 138
monumento 88
Monumento
    a Lincoln 89
Monumento
    a Washington 88
morado 7
morir 82
mosquito 119
motocicleta 70
mouse 44
muelle 72
muletas 74

multiplicar 158
muñeca 97
murciélago 120
músculo 98
museo 60
musgo 121
música 26

N

nacer 82
naranja 7
nariz 94
negro 7
Neptuno 153
nido 112
niebla 146
nieve 146
nivel 141
noche 6
noveno/a 4
noventa 3
noviembre 5
nube 148
Nueva York 89
nueve 2
nuevo/a 8
numerador 162
números enteros . . 162
números pares 158

O

observar 106
océano 84
ochenta 3
ocho 2
octavo/a 4
octubre 5
oficial de policía . . . 60
oficial de tránsito . . 36
oficina 37
oficina de correos . . 60

oído 101

oír 100

ojos 14

ola 148

oler 100, 101

once 2

onza 165

órbita 152

oreja 95

orificio para
  respirar 115

orquídea 121

oruga 112

oscuro 15

oso 118

P

p. m. 157

paciente 74

padre 16

padres 16

país 84, 86

pájaro 113

pájaro
  carpintero 119

pan 25

pantalones 28

pantalones cortos . 30

pañuelos de
  pape 150

papel 40, 150

parada de
  autobús 68

paraguas 30

paramédico 74

pared 18

párpado 94

parque 59

parrilla 130

partes iguales 162

pasta 102

pasto 12

pata 110

patear 48

patrulla de
  policía 70

pecho 96

pedir 67

pegamento 40

peinarse el
  cabello 12

peine 22

pelotas 48

península 138

pensar 34

pentágono 160

pequeño/a 8

pera 102

periódico 42

perro de las
  pradera 116

pesado/a 9

pescado 103

pestañas 14

pétalo 108

pezuña 111

piano 130

pico 110

pie 96, 164

piedrecita 142

piel 98, 110

pierna 96

pijama 28

pimientos 102

piña 64

piña 118

pino 118

pinta 164

pirámide 160

piso 19

pizarra 40

plancha 130

planetas 152

plano/a 145

planta de
  semillero 108

plástico 150, 150

plátanos 24

plato 24

pluma 38, 110

polen 109

polilla 120

pollito 113

pollo 66, 78

portero 37

precio 166

precipitación 149

predecir 126

presidente 86

prima 17

primavera 30

primero/a 4

prisma 130

probar 126

problema 158

proteger a la
  comunidad 57

púa 144

puente 72

puerta 18

pulgada 164

pulmones 98

pulpo 114

punto decimal 163

Q

queso 103

quince 2

quinto/a 4

quirófano 75

R

radio 26
radiografía 74
raíces. 108
rana. 112
rápido/a. 8
rascacielos 71
ratón 116
raya 114
rayas 89, 123
rayo 146
rebotar 48
recámara. 19
recepcionista 74
reciclar 151
recoger. 21, 79
recostarse 51
recta numérica . . . 158
rectángulo. 160
reflejo 131
refrigerador 24
registrar 126
regla de un metro. 107
regla 40, 106
reír 53
reloj 40
reloj despertador . . 20
remolcador. 72
renacuajo 112
reparar carros 56
repetir 34
resbaladilla. 132
responder
    preguntas 35
restar. 158
reunión. 87
revista 42
río 148
rizado/a 15
roble 118

rocas 142
rodar 132
rodilla 96
rojo. 7
rompecabezas. 21
ropa interior 28
rosa 108
rosa de los vientos . 85
rosado. 7
rotulador 38
ruedas. 132
ruidoso/a. 101

S

sábado. 5
sacapuntas. 38
sacar un libro 43
sala de espera 74
sala de estar. 18
sala de un tribunal. 86
sala de urgencias . . 74
salida 77
salir del cascarón . 113
salón de arte 37
salón de clases 37
salón de música . . . 37
saltar. 48
sandalias. 31
sándwich. 46
sangrar. 50
Saturno. 153
seco/a. 9, 23
secretaria. 36
segundo/a. 4
seis 2
seis menos
    cuarto 156
5:45 156
semáforo 60
semillas 108

señal de alto. 58
sentir 100
septiembre 5
séptimo/a 4
serpiente 116
servilleta 67
servir alimentos. . . . 56
sesenta. 3
setenta 3
sexto/a 4
siete 2
silbato. 130
silencioso/a. 101
silla. 40
silla de ruedas 74
símbolos. 85
Sistema Solar 152
smog. 150
sobre 10, 11
sofá 26
sol. 146
Sol 152
sólido 128
sombra. 131
sombrero 30
sonreír. 52
sopa. 66
sorprendido/a 52
suave. 100
sucio/a 9
sudadera 28
suéter 30
sumar 158
supermercado 62

T

tabla 127
tacto 100
tallo 108
tambor 130

tapete 26
tarde 6
tarjeta de la
   biblioteca 42
taxi 61
taza 24, 164
taza de medir 107
tazón 67
teclado 44
teléfono 26
telescopio 153
televisión 26
temperatura 146
tenedor 66
tenis 29
tentáculos 115
tercer/o/a 4
termómetro 50, 107
tía 17
tiburón 114
tienda de
   a barrotes 63
tierra 142
tigre 111
tijera 38
tina 22
tío 17
Tiranosaurio Rex . . 144
toalla 22
toallas de papel . . . 65
tobillo 96
tocador 20
tomacorriente 134
tomate 64, 109
tormenta
   eléctrica 146
tornado 147
tortuga 120
toser 51
trabajar con
   un compañero . . . 35

trabajar en
   grupo 35
tractor 78
traje de baño 31
trece 2
treinta 3
tren 70
trepar 49
tres 2
triángulo 160
tribunal 48, 87
Triceratops 145
triste 52
tronco 118
tulipán 108

U

un cuarto 162
un medio 162
un tercio 162
uña del dedo
   del pie 99
uña 99
uniforme 76
uno 2
Urano 153
usar pañuelos
   de papel 93
usar protector
   solar 93
uvas 24

V

vaca 78
vacío/a 9
valle 140
vapor 148
vegetales 103
veinte 2
veinticinco 3
veinticuatro 3

veintidós 3
veintitrés 3
veintiuno 3
vela 130
velero 72
venda 50
vendedor 62
vender ropa 56
vender 167
ventana 18
ventilador 134
ventisca 147
Venus 153
ver 100
verano 31
verde 7
verter 126
vestido 28
vestirse 12
vía de evacuación . 77
viajar 69
viajar 82
vidrio 150, 150
viejo/a 8
viento 146
viernes 5
vista 100
volcán 138, 143
votación 87
voto 87

Y

yarda 164
yeso74
yogur 102

Z

zanahorias 46
zapatería 62
zapatos 29